MINISTERIAL RESPONSIBILITY
FOR NATIONAL SECURITY

MINISTERIAL RESPONSIBILITY FOR NATIONAL SECURITY

as it relates to the Offices of Prime Minister, Attorney General and Solicitor General of Canada

by

Professor J. Ll. J. Edwards LL.D. (Cantab.)
of the Faculty of Law and Centre of Criminology
University of Toronto

Special Adviser to the Commission of Inquiry
Concerning Certain Activities of the
Royal Canadian Mounted Police

The Prime Minister has approved the publication of this study in advance of the final report of the Commission.

Catalogue No. CP 32-38/1980-3E   Canada: $5.25
ISBN 0-660-10501-2   Other countries: $6.30

A Note by the Commissioners

An important part of the terms of reference of our Commission of Inquiry (P.C. 1977-1911) reads as follows:

(a)   to advise and make such report as the Commissioners deem necessary and desirable in the interest of Canada, regarding the policies and procedures governing the activities of the R.C.M.P. in the discharge of its responsibility to protect the security of Canada, the means to implement such policies and procedures, as well as the adequacy of the laws of Canada as they apply to such policies and procedures, having regard to the needs of the security of Canada.

Professor Edwards' study discusses many important issues that have a bearing on this aspect of our terms of reference. Indeed, while the opinions he expresses are his own and not necessarily those of the Commission or of the Government of Canada, we hope that his paper will provoke and stimulate the reader to express his or her own considered views to the Commission by writing to it at:

P.O. Box 1982
Station B
Ottawa, Ontario
KIP 5R5

Mr. Justice D.C. McDonald (*Chairman*)

D.S. Rickerd, Q.C.

G. Gilbert, Q.C.

v

Table of Contents

Preface

A few words of explanation are necessary in introducing this study. It was prepared at the invitation of the Commission of Inquiry concerning certain activities of the Royal Canadian Mounted Police, a title which tends to belie the full scope of the inquiry which is that of the overall security of Canada. Hence the title that I have given to this work. Whilst the principal emphasis is placed on the political responsibilities of the three Ministers of the Crown, including the Prime Minister of Canada, who, by the nature of their offices, are most closely associated with the activities of the R.C.M.P. Security Service, the study endeavours to examine the troublesome questions that arise in this relatively unexplored area of government against both a historical and comparative background. By virtue of our early history it is inevitable that the treatment of these questions leans heavily on British constitutional law and practice. At the same time, attention is directed to the experience of such countries as the United States and Australia which have been engrossed during the 1970's in subjecting their nation's security services to the same intensive scrutiny as the present Commission of Inquiry is undertaking with respect to Canada. Hopefully, the insights that I have derived from these international parallels will assist the reader in gaining a better grasp of what should be expected of its parliament, its ministers and its police and security forces in maintaining the nation's security.

The first substantial draft of this monograph was presented to the Commission of Inquiry in August 1978, since which time I have had the immense benefit of comments by a number of friends and colleagues whose acquaintanceship with the subject matter of this work has inevitably been that of scholars not practitioners. Whatever may be the eventual recommendations of the Commissioners, the ensuing study demonstrates the need for a better understanding of the fragile machinery we have in place to ensure effective political responsibility for everything that is done in the name of national security.

The views and conclusions that I have expressed are entirely my own and are not to be read as in any way committing the Government of Canada or the Commission of Inquiry to the positions expressed in this work. Likewise no responsibility for the final contents of what follows should be attributed to those who were kind enough to respond to my request for comments on the study. Their responses were invariably helpful and ensured that I directed my mind to many underlying issues that, on first acquaintance, I may have overlooked or dealt with inadequately. In this regard I particularly would like to thank the following friends and colleagues: Professor A.W. Bradley, Faculty of Law, University of Edinburgh; Mr. A.J.E. Brennan, Deputy Under Secretary of State, Home Office, England; Mr. Gordon Dodds, Public Archives of Canada; Mr. K.T. Fuad, Director, Legal Division, Commonwealth Secretariat, London; Mr. Graham Kelly, Legal Counsellor, Australian Embassy, Washington; Mr. Geoffrey Marshall, Fellow of Queen's College, Oxford; Professor A.W. Mewett, Faculty of Law, University of Toronto; Professor Peter Russell, Department of Political Economy, University of Toronto and Research Director to the Commission of Inquiry; Mr. Philip Stenning, Centre of Criminology, University of Toronto; Mr. Harold B. Tyler Jr., formerly Deputy Attorney General of the United States; Mr. D.G.T. Williams, Fellow of Emmanuel College, Cambridge; and Professor Graham Zellick, Visiting Professor, Faculty of Law, University of Toronto.

Every attempt has been made to take into account Canadian and international developments between August 1978 and September 1979, when the final text was submitted to the McDonald Commission of Inquiry. I have deliberately refrained from incorporating, or making any observations on, the public testimony given before the Commission by former Ministers of the Crown and other witnesses on matters that pertain to the subjects dealt with in this study. The only exception to this approach involves the public statements regarding the changes to the Security Service's internal audit machinery which have been approved by the Commissioner of the R.C.M.P., and which bear directly on one of the important aspects of ministerial responsibility.

A final word of sincere thanks is due to my son Mark Edwards, student-at-law, who was my research assistant during the early stages of this work.

J.Ll.J. Edwards

September 25, 1979.

1. Public confusion as to the unique role of the Law Officers in Government

The statute law which has emerged from the Parliament of Canada since 1867, and the Legislatures of the Provinces since 1885, expressly confirms the lineage of the federal and provincial offices of the Attorney General and the Solicitor General in Canada. In enactment after enactment the identical provision is to be found conferring upon the Canadian Law Officers of the Crown the same powers and duties that belong by law or usage to the offices of Attorney General and Solicitor General of England and Wales, insofar as these functions are applicable to the particular jurisdiction in Canada. This caveat is no mere matter of words, since there have been significant differences between the two countries in the development of these important offices of State, differences that continue to exert a marked influence on the interpretation of the constitutional role to be performed by the Attorney General or the Solicitor General, as the case may be.

During the early period of Canadian history when direct colonial rule was being exercised, as well as throughout the years leading up to responsible government, the holders of the offices of Attorney General and Solicitor General used their official positions in pursuit of political purposes to a degree that has never been evident in the relationship between the English Law Officers and the government of the day. The advent of Confederation did little to change the belief that the Attorney General, by virtue of his membership in the Cabinet of the federal and provincial governments, is subject to the same doctrine of collective responsibility as that of his ministerial colleagues. One of the principal theses to be developed in this paper is that such an approach is misconceived and seriously damaging to the independent exercise of the Attorney General's responsibilities especially in the area of criminal prosecutions.

More recently, Canada has resorted to using the office of Solicitor General for purposes connected with the police and law enforcement that are totally foreign to the basic conception of the role associated with the Solicitor General in Britain. This creates its own problems when defining the nature and extent of the Solicitor General's accountability to Parliament (or a Provincial legislature) for the activities of the police forces and security services that fall within the ambit of his portfolio. There is no necessity for Canadian practice to slavishly adhere to the law and conventions that govern the exercise of the Law Officers' functions in England, and which have been developed over the six centuries that these offices have been in existence. It cannot be denied, however, that the recent departures from the British constitutional model have introduced elements of confusion in interpreting the limits and responsibilities of the office of Solicitor General of Canada. Some consolation may be found

1

in the fact that the Canadian experience is not wholly exceptional in this regard.

In view of the regrettable absence of published writings on the role of the offices of Attorney General and Solicitor General in Canadian constitutional history, perhaps I may be forgiven for referring at the outset of this study to some thoughts that I expressed not so long ago at the 1977 meeting in Winnipeg of the Commonwealth Law Ministers and Attorneys General. In a discussion paper prepared for that conference, entitled "Emerging problems in defining the modern role of the office of Attorney General in Commonwealth countries", a copy of which is attached to this study (Appendix A), I wrote: "If my assumption is correct that there exists throughout every country of the Commonwealth a vast body of public ignorance as to the essential role and functions of the office of Attorney General, part of the blame for this state of affairs must rest with past and present holders of the portfolios and offices represented at this meeting. Reading the parliamentary debates, journals and newspapers of the respective Commonwealth countries evinces little of substance by way of public explanation of the office of Attorney General or its special responsibilities as the avowed guardian of the public interest. This situation needs to be rectified. In saying this, I hasten to acknowledge the efforts and example of those few incumbents who have done a great deal in this regard, and their positions of independence have been commensurately strengthened. There remains, however, the ongoing task of educating all sections of society, not the least of these being the members of legislative assemblies and members of the legal profession, as to the powers and restraints that must constantly engage the Attorney General in making decisions that lie at the very heart of the administration of justice."[1]

This plea did not go unheeded. In their final communique, also attached (Appendix B), the Commonwealth Law Ministers declared that: "In order to dispel public misunderstanding in the matter, Ministers considered that practical measures might be taken by governments throughout the Commonwealth to improve political, governmental and general public awareness of the unique role of the Attorney General's office."[2] It is no coincidence that, when the opportunity arose recently, arising out of the *Cossitt* affair in the House of Commons and the exercise of the Attorney General's fiat under the Official Secrets Act, to explain his decision to institute criminal proceedings against the Toronto Sun, its publisher and editor but not against the Member of Parliament concerned, the Attorney General of Canada, Mr. Ron Basford, chose to elaborate extensively on the nature of his office and his accountability to Parliament for the exercise of his ministerial discretion.[3] No comparable statement will be found in the annals of the Canadian House of Commons, in itself a remarkable state of affairs.

It requires little imagination to anticipate that the contents of Mr. Basford's statement to the Commons on March 17, 1973 will be cited in future years as the *locus classicus* both with respect to the exercise of the Attorney General of Canada's prosecutorial discretion and also the ambit of ministerial responsibility as it relates to the Law Officers in Canada. In the sphere of the provincial administration of justice it was no coincidence that, around the same time, the Attorney General of Ontario provided the Legislative Assembly with an elaborate explanation of his decision not to launch a prosecution against Mr. Francis Fox, the former Solicitor General of Canada, arising out of circumstances having nothing to do with the minister's official duties.[4]

Such statements are bound to have a beneficial effect on public understanding of the special nature of the office of Attorney General and of the delicate balance that must constantly be maintained between the independent exercise of his "public interest" functions and the application of the doctrine of individual ministerial responsibility. The welcome appearance of these ministerial pronouncements, containing fully developed reasons for decisions in cases that were very much in the public eye, should not obscure the realities of the past in which, more often than not, Prime Ministers and Ministers alike showed less than a clear grasp of the constitutional limits of ministerial accountability as it relates to the Law Officers of the Crown. Furthermore, it is not surprising that difficulties are being experienced at the present time in defining the scope of the Solicitor General's accountability to Parliament where the situations being questioned arise from the exercise of functions, viz., policing and the security services, that, in terms of history and tradition, have had no place in the appointment from which the Canadian office of Solicitor General is derived.

2. Functions of the Minister of Justice and Attorney General of Canada — evolution and legislation

Before proceeding to examine the historical development of the offices of Attorney General and Solicitor General in England and Wales, with particular reference to the constitutional conventions that govern their accountability to Parliament, it may be well to state the legal foundations on which the powers and functions of their Canadian counterparts are said to rest. Unlike most modern constitutions within the Commonwealth, the British North America Act, 1867, is somewhat unhelpful in this regard. Executive power is declared "to continue and be vested in the Queen" (s.9). The Executive Council, to aid and advise in the Government of Canada, is to consist of "persons who... shall be from time to time chosen and summoned by the Governor General and sworn in as Privy Councillors, and members thereof may be from time to time removed by the Governor General" (s.11). No specific reference is made in the Act to the portfolios that would initially comprise the Executive Council of the Dominion Government, but there can be no doubt that, following the pattern established since the advent of British rule in Canada, it was envisaged that the Attorney General would be included. Neither would it have occasioned surprise at the time, in 1867, that the first Canadian Prime Minister, Sir John A. Macdonald, elected to join the duties of the Attorney General with his responsibilities as First Minister.

The British North America Act is more precise when dealing with executive power in the provincial constitutions. The Attorney General, according to section 63, heads the list of executive officers named as initially constituting the Executive Council in the provinces of Ontario and Quebec. This provision confirmed the long established tradition which had prevailed from the earliest days of colonial rule in the Province of Quebec. Commencing with the period preceding the conquest of New France, when Paris was the seat of the prevailing colonial power, the Attorney General was an ex-officio member of the Sovereign Council.[5] With the subsequent institution of British colonial rule, a succession of English lawyers were appointed to the office of Attorney General in the distant colony and participated actively, alongside the Governor, in determining and executing policies within the mandate laid down by Whitehall. Another integral member of the Governor's Council, throughout almost the entire period of colonial rule, was the Chief Justice, there being scarcely any recognition of the innate conflict of interest that such a move would evoke at the present day.

With the division, following the Quebec Act, 1774, of the former province into Upper and Lower Canada, the practice of including the Attorney General

5

within the small body of persons selected by the colonial Governor to advise him in administering the government was continued. The minutes of that body in Upper Canada show how actively the two legal members, the Chief Justice and the Attorney General, participated in the deliberations of the Executive Council.[6] By the time the British North America Act, 1867 was enacted the imperative need to separate the judiciary from the executive and legislative branches of government had been fully recognized. The position of the Attorney General, however, as a key figure in the executive councils of the expanding confederation remained unchanged and it is of notable significance that the office to this day is regarded as one of the most senior Cabinet posts in both the federal and provincial governments. Whether this constitutional practice should endure is a question that will be examined more closely later in this paper. At that time we shall have occasion also to evaluate the role and functions of the office of Solicitor General, with particular reference to its recent emergence, in Ottawa and in the provinces of Ontario and Alberta, as the minister responsible for policing and law enforcement. It will suffice for the moment to note that in the same section 63 of the British North America Act, which reinforced the status of the Attorney General as the ranking member of the Executive Councils of Ontario and Quebec, special reference is made to the inclusion within the Executive Council of Quebec of the Solicitor General and the Speaker of the Legislative Council.

Following the enactment of the British North America Act constituting the new Dominion, and in furtherance of sections 91 and 92 delineating the distribution of legislative powers within Confederation, the Parliament of Canada in 1868 enacted the first statute respecting the Department of Justice.[7] Its principal components, apart from the significant changes introduced in 1966 when a new Department of the Solicitor General was established, remain as operative today as when the statute was originally promulgated. It may be advisable, therefore, to set forth the provisions of the 1868 enactment in full with a note of such changes as have been effected in the form or substance of the contemporary statute regulating the federal Department of Justice. Thus, section 1 of the 1868 Act provides:

> "There shall be a Department of the Civil Service of Canada, to be called 'The Department of Justice' over which the Minister of Justice of Canada, for the time being, appointed by the Governor by Commission under the Great Seal, and who shall, *ex officio*, be Her Majesty's Attorney General of Canada, shall preside; and the said Minister of Justice shall hold office during pleasure and shall have the management and direction of the Department of Justice."

There has been some tidying up in the opening sections of the enactment bearing the same title in the Revised Statutes of Canada, 1970, c.J-2, but the essentials remain. The familiar phraseology denoting the responsibility of the Minister of Justice for "the management and direction of the Department of Justice" brooks no doubt as to which Minister of the Crown Parliament must look for answers to questions relating to the activities of the Department. There exists only the one portfolio, that of the Minister of Justice, though the clear assignment *ex-officio* to the Minister of the duties and responsibilities of the Attorney General of Canada gives every appearance of dual portfolios. This is not so, though in 1878 a Bill was passed through the Commons, after a lengthy debate, authorising the establishment of a separate portfolio of the

Attorney General of Canada, with a seat in the Cabinet in his own right.[8] Parliament was dissolved before the Bill reached the statute book. That measure envisaged the Attorney General presiding jointly with the Minister of Justice over what was then described as the Law Department. Speaking as the Leader of the Opposition, Sir John A. Macdonald argued strongly against the Bill on the grounds that confusion would reign in the Cabinet if it had two law ministers proffering advice.[9] Macdonald preferred the alternative course of creating an office of Solicitor General of Canada who would assist the Minister of Justice and be a member of the Administration but not hold Cabinet rank.[10] As we shall see later, Sir John A. Macdonald was to be instrumental in effectuating this change in 1837, all stages of the legislation being fulfilled by the House of Commons in a single day.[11]

To revert to the terms of the 1868 Act respecting the Department of Justice, it should be noted that the separation of the respective duties of the Minister of Justice and the Attorney General of Canada is not simply a matter of tidy draftsmanship. Incidentally, no less a figure than Sir John A. Macdonald himself is attributed with drafting the historic measure.[12] Embedded within the provisions, set out below, are the strains of an inherited set of principles that must be kept constantly in the forefront of the Minister's mind if he is not to fall into the trap that brought about the downfall in 1965 of the then Minister of Justice, Mr. Guy Favreau. More of that event later.[13] According to section 2 of the 1968 enactment:

"The duties of the Minister of Justice shall be as follows: He shall be the legal member of Her Majesty's Privy Council for Canada; It shall be his duty to see that the administration of public affairs is in accordance with law; He shall have the superintendence of all matters connected with the administration of justice in Canada, not within the jurisdiction of the Government of the Provinces and composing the same; He shall advise upon the Legislative Acts and proceedings of each of the Legislatures of the Provinces of Canada, and generally advise the Crown upon all matters of law referred to him by the Crown; and he shall be charged generally with such other duties as may at any time be assigned by the Governor-in-Council to the Minister of Justice."

Up to the present day there has been no change in this recital of the Minister's responsibilities. Concurrently, the duties of the Attorney General of Canada, as set out in section 3 of the Department of Justice Act 1868, provide as follows:

"He shall be entrusted with the powers and charged with the duties which belong to the office of the Attorney General of England by law or usage as far as the same powers and duties are applicable to Canada, and also with the powers and duties which by the laws of the several Provinces belonged to the office of Attorney General of each Province up to the time when the Laws under the provisions of the said Act are to be administered and carried into effect by the Government of the Dominion; He shall advise the Heads of the several Departments of the Government upon all matters of Law connected with such Departments; He shall be charged with the settlement and approval of all instruments issued under the Great Seal of Canada; He shall have the superintendence of Penitentiaries and the Prison System of the Dominion; He shall have the regulation and conduct of all litigation for or against the Crown or any Public Department, in respect of any subjects within the authority or jurisdiction of the Dominion; and he shall be charged generally with such other duties as may at anytime be assigned by the Governor-in-Council to the Attorney General of Canada."

Several observations suggest themselves in reviewing the above recital of the duties and powers of the Minister of Justice and Attorney General of Canada, especially as they distinguish the Canadian Law Minister's functions from those exercisable by his British counterparts. As is well known, English constitutional law has never formally recognised the existence of a Minister of Justice, preferring instead to adhere to its distribution of the broad range of functions connected with the administration of justice and the maintenance of law and order between the Lord Chancellor's Department, the Home Office and the Law Officers' Department. In brief, the Lord Chancellor's responsibilities include the judiciary and the courts. As a senior member of the Cabinet he is also the principal legal adviser of the Government, and presides over the House of Lords as well as acting, from time to time, as government spokesman in the Upper House. His role as Speaker of the House of Lords apart, it is fair to state that the Lord Chancellor and the Minister of Justice of Canada have many duties in common and that the unifying elements outnumber the differences between the two offices.

It is in his capacity as Minister of Justice, and not as the Attorney General of Canada, that the incumbent is accorded his seat as the legal member of the Privy Council and of the Cabinet. By virtue of his position in the Administration, the Minister of Justice is looked upon as the principal adviser of the Crown and of the Government of Canada. It is difficult, however, if not wholly unrealistic, to make much of the distinction drawn by the Act of 1868 in circumscribing the advisory role of the Attorney General, *qua* Attorney General, to that of advising the Heads of Department, as opposed to the Government itself, upon all matters of law connected with such Departments. Whilst the question of settling and approving instruments issued under the Great Seal of Canada figures prominently in the minutes of the early Executive Council in Upper Canada, where the contentious issue of fees for the Law Officers was repeatedly at stake, the retention of this function by the Attorney General of Canada is now mainly of historical interest.

In view of statements made later by Mr. Cardin, the Minister of Justice at the time of the major separation in 1966, attention must be drawn to the inclusion of the heading "superintendence of penitentiaries and prisons in the Dominion" within the list of original duties associated with the Attorney General of Canada, functions, it may be added, that would be regarded as totally alien to the office of Attorney General in England. In that country, prisons, parole and correctional services have always been the concern of the Home Secretary. A major area of identity between the English and Canadian distribution of functions in the administration of justice is the expectation that the Attorney General will be responsible for the conduct of all litigation for or against the Crown or any public department.

The absence of any reference to the police and policing functions in the Department of Justice Act, 1868, is readily explained by the prevailing circumstances. In addition to his duties as Prime Minister and Minister of Justice from 1867 to 1873, Sir John A. Macdonald personally assumed responsibility for overseeing the reorganisation of the North West Mounted Police.[14] From the first statute of 1873 regulating the police force in the North West Territories, and its successors the Royal Northwest Mounted Police and the Royal Canadian Mounted Police, the same formula is to be found placing the Commissioner of the force "subject to the control, orders and authority of such person or persons as may, from time to time, be named by the Governor-in-Council for that purpose"[15] or saying "such member of the King's Privy Council for Canada as the Governor-in-Council from time to time directs, shall have the control and management of the Force and of all matters connected therewith."[16] Although, as we have seen, the Department of Justice Act, 1868, was totally silent on the subject of policing, the predominant role that this department was to play in the affairs of the federal police force was first enunciated in 1873, only five years after the inception of the Department of Justice. Thus, the North West Mounted Police Act, 1873, provided that:

> "The Department of Justice shall have the control and management of the Police and all matters connected therewith: but the Governor-in-Council may, at any time, order that the same shall be transferred to any other Department of the Civil Service of Canada..."[17]

Such a transfer of responsibility — it is surmised that it was of a temporary nature — appears to have taken place in 1878 when the Secretary of State was designated as the responsible minister.[18]

This act of expediency, whatever its origins, should not cloud the realization that for nearly the entire first century of the federal police force's existence its constitutional home was the Department of Justice, a fact that was statutorily reaffirmed in 1959 in the R.C.M.P. Act of that year[19] which expressly recognized the Minister of Justice as the Minister to whom the Commissioner of the R.C.M.P. was directly accountable.

This association terminated in 1966 with the placing on the statute book of the Government Organization Act, which provided that: "The duties, powers and functions of the Solicitor General of Canada extend to, and include, all matters over which the Parliament of Canada has jurisdiction, not by law assigned to any other department, branch or agency of the Government of Canada, relating to ... (c) the Royal Canadian Mounted Police".[20] Further confirmation of the new relationship that was instituted in 1966 between the federal police force and the Solicitor General of Canada is to be found in the Royal Canadian Mounted Police Act, 1970. There we find the language of the R.C.M.P. Act, 1959, s.5, being repeated in the 1970 enactment which states:

> "The Governor-in-Council may appoint an officer to be known as the Commissioner of the Royal Canadian Mounted Police who, under the direction of the Minister, has the control and management of the force and all matters connected therewith."[21]

The interpretation provisions in the 1970 statute further declare that wherever any reference is made in the Act to the "Minister" it is intended to refer to the Solicitor General of Canada.[22] Here then is to be found the explicit recognition of the modern day application of the doctrine of ministerial responsibility to all aspects of the Royal Canadian Mounted Police and of the ministerial role assigned by Parliament to the Solicitor General of Canada.

3. The office of provincial Attorney General — roots and legislative formulation of duties

It is not my intention in this study to advert at length to the constitutional issues that recently engaged the attention of the Supreme Court of Canada in *R* v. *Hauser et al.*[23] with respect to the prosecutorial powers, respectively, of the Attorney General of Canada and the provincial Attorneys General. At the heart of the running dispute between the federal and provincial Law Officers of the Crown is the 1968-69 amendment to the definition of "Attorney General" in section 2 of the Criminal Code.[24] According to the federal Department Justice the amendment re-affirmed the right of the Attorney General of Canada to institute criminal prosecutions not only with respect to federal statutory offences but also, in appropriate circumstances, crimes encompassed within the Criminal Code. It had been widely anticipated that an authoritative ruling on the question by the Supreme Court of Canada would have been forthcoming in the case of *Hauser*, which involved an appeal against a prohibition granted by the Appellate Division of the Supreme Court of Alberta requiring any judge of the District Court to abstain from trying a case launched by the agent of the Attorney General of Canada charging the accused with offences under the Narcotic Control Act, 1970, a federal statute. The constitutional question, as settled by Chief Justice Laskin, confined the argument before the Supreme Court to the following issues:[25]

> "Is it within the competence of the Parliament of Canada to enact legislation as in section 2 of the Criminal Code to authorize the Attorney General of Canada or his Agent
> (1) to prefer indictments for an offence under the Narcotic Control Act,
> (2) to have the conduct of proceedings instituted at the instance of the Government of Canada in respect of a violation or conspiracy to violate any Act of the Parliament of Canada or regulations made thereunder other than the Criminal Code".

By thus circumscribing the breadth of the appeal, the larger question of jurisdiction in respect to prosecuting offences under the Criminal Code was not resolved in *Hauser*, and remains to be determined in another case. It is unlikely to be left in abeyance for long.

Within the confines of the questions posed, the Supreme Court by a majority of 5 to 2,[26] upheld the claim of the Attorney General of Canada to exclusive jurisdiction, it being generally acknowledged that the issue of constitutionality was to be resolved according to whether the Narcotic Control Act was part of "criminal law strictly so called", under section 91(27) of the British North America Act, or a federal enactment which did not derive its constitutional validity from the same source in the 1867 statute. Drawing this dividing line in individual cases can sometimes severely test the credibility of the judicial analysis. The judgments in *Hauser* are no exception in this regard.

11

The contentious provisions in the B.N.A. Act, 1867, as is well known, are the areas of power contained in sections 91(27) and 92(14), the contents of which read as follows:

> S.91(27) "The Criminal Law, except the Constitution of Courts of Criminal Jurisdiction, but including the Procedure in Criminal Matters."
>
> S.92(14) "The Administration of Justice in the Province, including the Constitution, Maintenance, and Organization of Provincial Courts, both of Civil and of Criminal Jurisdiction, and including Procedure in Civil Matters in those Courts."

Invoking what he described as a trite statement of a fundamental principle of Canadian constitutional law, Spence J., claimed that federal legislative powers under section 91 of the B.N.A. Act are conferred upon Parliament exclusively, notwithstanding anything in that Act and particularly section 92 thereof. He went on to say:

> "Acting upon such a power Parliament has, throughout the Criminal Code, granted jurisdiction to various provincial courts and has imposed duties and has conferred powers on various provincial officials including, of course, the Attorneys General of the provinces. Those provincial courts in exercising such jurisdiction and those Attorneys General and other provincial officials in discharging their duties so imposed and exercising their powers so conferred do so by virtue of the federal legislation enacted under the enumerated head no. 27 of section 91 of the British North America Act."[27]

The learned judge's brief excursus into the history of criminal prosecutions and the role of the Attorney General before Confederation is set forth in the passage of his judgment wherein he states:

> "Prior to Confederation, however, the Attorneys General acted under their common law jurisdiction or as directed by the valid legislation of the particular colony. After Confederation they do so as empowered and directed by valid federal legislation. I can see no bar to Parliament, in the discharge of its valid legislative power, providing that as to certain duties or procedures the provincial officials shall not be used exclusively but the power may also be exercised by a federal official who may be the Attorney General of Canada or any investigating or prosecuting agency designated by Parliament."[28]

Since the *Hauser* appeal was decided, Spence J., has retired from the Supreme Court. Had he remained a member it is not difficult to perceive his stance on the broader constitutional question associated with the expanded definition of "Attorney General" introduced into the Criminal Code by the 1968-69 amendment.

This narrow, literalist approach to the interpretation of the key provisions in the British North America Act, advanced by counsel representing the Attorney General of Canada, was regarded as conferring upon the federal power jurisdiction to conduct *all* criminal proceedings. Such a view of the constitutional provisions was strenuously opposed by the Provinces. They found a staunch champion in the minority judgment delivered by Dickson, J. In the course of his expansive analysis of every aspect of the broad constitutional question, which lay just beneath the narrow issue determined in *Hauser*, Dickson, J., declared:

"... there are a number of federal offences which rely for their constitutional validity upon s.91 (27), the criminal law power, which are not found in the Criminal Code. That is to say, there are a number of federal non-Code "criminal" offences. The effect of the last clause in s.2(2), along with the Interpretation Act, is to extend the Attorney General of Canada's potential role as "Attorney General" to all federal offences whether found in the Criminal Code or not. For the purposes of the constitutional question, this has vital implications. If s.2(2), as it now stands, is found within the powers of the federal government, then it is manifest that there is nothing to stop the federal government from similarly restricting the powers of the provincial Attorney General within the confines of the Criminal Code itself or, indeed, of stripping provincial Attorneys General of all Code powers. That is the "broad proposition" candidly advanced on behalf of the federal Crown in these proceedings. The constitutional issue does not respect the artificial barriers established by terming a piece of legislation "the Criminal Code," but directs the inquiry to the criminal law power of s.91(27) of the British North America Act, 1867."[29]

The nub of the conflict, according to Dickson, J., "is not over the right of Parliament to enforce its own enactments but rather, and this bears repeated emphasis, the attempt by Parliament to exclude the provinces from the right to supervise criminal prosecutions".[30]

In other cases determined by provincial Courts of Appeal,[31] it was pointed out, considerable support was forthcoming for the notion of concurrent jurisdiction as between the federal and provincial Attorneys General as a means of resolving the conflict. Dickson, J., would have nothing to do with this solution, stating:

"Because of the effects of paramountcy, the result of declaring concurrent jurisdiction is, so far as the office of provincial Attorney General is concerned in relation to prosecution of criminal offences, the same as a declaration of exclusive federal power. Whether one speaks in terms of federal power, or of concurrency, the provincial power, being subservient, must give way. There can never be two Attorneys General in respect of the same proceeding. Acceptance of the notion of concurrency would have the effect of removing from the provincial Attorney General the primary right and duty to prosecute in the Province."[32]

In the end, the learned judge concluded, the constitutional question is reduced to the drawing of a firm line between exclusive federal and provincial jurisdictions or, expressed differently, the allocation of the subject matter in question to one or other level of government.

Dickson, J., alone of the Supreme Court judges, devoted considerable attention to the historical development of the machinery of prosecutions in Canada, and correctly pointed out that the Provinces had exclusively supervised the administration of criminal justice, including prosecutions, prior to the enactment of the British North America Act, 1867, and, so far as the prosecution of Criminal Code offences was concerned, without any challenge by the federal Attorney General until the 1968-69 amendment, referred to earlier. The enactment of that amendment, according to Dickson, J.,

"...may be viewed as not only an attempt to intrude into matters traditionally reserved for the provincial Attorneys General, but also as a breach of the bargain struck at the time of Confederation. No practical reasons have been advanced for setting aside the practices and customs of one hundred years."[33]

Here is the embodiment of the "Confederation compact" approach to the interpretation of the B.N.A. Act. Having launched his well deployed arsenal of arguments rejecting the basic premise of the Attorney General of Canada, Dickson, J. terminated his minority judgment by saying:

> "The inescapable conclusion to be drawn from the legislative history, governmental attitudes, and case law is that the supervisory functions of the Attorney General in the administration of criminal justice have been considered to fall to the provinces under section 91(27)."[33A]

The lines of the festering dispute having been drawn in the *Hauser* case we must await the final outcome of the struggle between the federal and provincial Law Officers of the Crown to the time when the constitutional question is framed in a manner that will not permit any further circumvention.

Without in any way prejudging the ultimate disposition of this constitutional tug-of-war, it should not escape notice that many former Ministers of Justice and Attorneys General of Canada, when challenged in the House of Commons to explain apparent inactivity on their part in matters of prosecuting crimes, have repeatedly defended their position by reminding Members of Parliament that the question of instituting criminal proceedings under provisions of the Criminal Code is primarily a decision for the provincial Attorney General concerned to make. At least this was so until March, 1977 when, in reply to a question as to the constitutionality of the amendment to section 2 of the Criminal Code, the Minister of Justice, Mr. Ron Basford stated:[34] "The view of most of the [provincial] Attorneys General, and we have discussed this on many occasions is that there is, or should be, no prosecutorial role for the Attorney General of Canada. This is a position I do not accept". John Turner adopted a different stance in 1969 when he presided over the federal Department of Justice. In response to challenges by the Opposition that, as Minister of Justice and Attorney General of Canada, he should take action with respect to the alleged revolutionary conduct of some members of the Company of Young Canadians based in Montreal, Mr. Turner stated:[35] "The decision on whether a prosecution should be taken properly lies with the Attorney General of Quebec. The right honourable gentleman [Mr. Diefenbaker] is talking about subversion, sedition and this sort of thing and quite properly so. I have searched the records and at no time since Confederation has a prosecution for sedition been taken by the federal Attorney General. Sedition is a crime under the Criminal Code of Canada and in this, as in all other matters, prosecutions taken under the Criminal Code are taken by the provincial Attorney General". A few weeks later Mr. Turner corrected his earlier statement, and admitted that a file had been found in the Department of Justice indicating that in 1919, arising out of the Winnipeg general strike, prosecutions for seditious conspiracy were launched by counsel retained by the then Minister of Justice, Arthur Meighen. Even so, John Turner maintained, "The error... does not change the basic point I was trying to establish viz., that the prime responsibility for enforcing prosecutions for sedition under the Criminal Code is provincial".[36]

Mr. Turner was to adhere to this position during the tumultuous debates in the Commons in connection with the 1970 FLQ crisis,[37] and, it will be recalled, in the earliest Parliamentary debates concerning the activities of the Royal Canadian Mounted Police, which are said to have taken place around the same period, the Government's spokesmen repeatedly emphasised that the proper procedure was being followed in submitting any factual evidence of wrongdoing to the Attorney General of Quebec for him to make decisions as to the laying of criminal charges.[38]

Historically, there can be no room for doubt that above all the duties associated with the office of Attorney General in the pre-Confederation period was the exclusive responsibility for making prosecutorial decisions and, until other governmental distractions came to occupy more and more of the Attorney General's energies, to actually conduct the more serious prosecutions on behalf of the Crown.[39] The exercise of this particular function derived its authority from the Royal prerogative and, as has been reflected repeatedly in the decisions of the courts, is not amenable to judicial supervision as to the grounds upon which the Attorney General's discretion was based.[40] It will be necessary to enlarge on this proposition later. That being so, it becomes even more important to understand the role of the Legislative Assembly, following upon the advent of responsible government, in holding the Attorney General accountable to it for his decisions in the field of criminal prosecutions.

Before responsible government became a reality the Attorney General was very much an instrument of the Governor and the Executive Council with, occasionally, instances of direct intervention by the Colonial Secretary either on his own initiative or in response to a call for clarification of his duties by the Attorney General on the local scene.[41] If such indications suggest the antithesis of independence in the fulfillment of the Attorney General's prerogative powers it must, nevertheless, be acknowledged as a correct description. The present day holders of the office of provincial Attorney General would find considerable difficulty in subscribing to the interpretation of its functions that prevailed during the period when appointments to the offices of Attorney General and Solicitor General in the colonies were controlled by Whitehall and the incumbents were English barristers.

The essential feature to note in this short account of the early development of the office of Attorney General in Canada is the context within which the powers and duties of the Law Officers were executed in the distant colony. Direct rule prevailed and both the Attorney General and Solicitor General, for the time being, owed their appointments to, sometimes, the Governor, and often, on a more personal basis, the Secretary of State for the Colonies himself. Resistance to outside interventions began to exhibit itself with the emergence of Canadian born lawyers trained in Canada rather than in the English Inns of Court. This feeling of not wishing to be dependent upon, or subservient to, the colonial authorities in London figures more prominently in the minds of the Law Officers during the period of representative government in Upper Canada. Throughout those years and later the Attorney General and Solicitor General of the day sought to pattern their approach to

15

the prerogative powers associated with their offices on the example set by the Attorney General and Solicitor General of England. This determination to conform to the precedents established by the English Law Officers, at least in theory, can be said to prevail to the present day and we find positive expression of the reasons for this attitude in the statutes that currently exist in all the provinces defining the provincial Attorney General's powers and duties.

What is interesting to observe is that the older colonies, the original member provinces of Confederation, chose to continue, for many years after 1867, to rely upon the conventions and customs that had prevailed in their jurisdictions before the new Dominion was brought into existence. The precise definition of these constitutional practices, from the earliest days following the conquest of Quebec to the advent of responsible government, must be traced through the Commissions of Appointment, the Governor's Instructions, memorials to the Colonial Office by individual Law Officers and other correspondence that passed between the colony's senior administrative officials and their governors in London. This is obviously a major exercise well beyond the scope of the present paper but it is to this voluminous body of records, fortunately preserved in the English Public Record Office and in our own National and Provincial Archives, that attention must be directed if we are to document with accuracy the various stages in the development of the office of the provincial Attorney General. Thus, Upper Canada and Lower Canada, as well as the provinces of Nova Scotia and New Brunswick, persisted, long after the newer provinces had resorted to legislation to spell out the functions of the Attorney General in their jurisdiction, in relying upon the readily available precedents of earlier years in defining the prerogative limits of the provincial Law Officers of the Crown.

Furthermore, so far as Ontario and Quebec are concerned, the British North America Act has expressly confirmed the prerogative powers of the Attorney General and Solicitor General of those provinces, section 135 stating:

> "Until the Legislature of Ontario or Quebec otherwise provides, all Rights, Powers, Duties, Functions, Responsibilities, or Authorities at the passing of this Act vested in or imposed on the Attorney General, Solicitor General, ... by any Law, Statute, or Ordinance of Upper Canada, Lower Canada, or Canada, and not repugnant to this Act, shall be vested in or imposed on any Officer to be appointed by the Lieutenant Governor for the Discharge of the same or any of them."

Interim legislative sanction, until the respective legislatures saw fit to make alternative arrangements for such appointments under the Great Seal of the Provinces of Ontario or Quebec, was afforded by section 134 of the same statute. That provision extended, in the case of the office of Solicitor General, to Quebec alone. To revert to the more general language of section 135 of the British North America Act, 1867, it is significant that in *R. v. Pontbriand* (1978)[42] Hugessen A.C.J. of the Quebec Superior Court invoked its provisions when interpreting the terms of ss. 91(27) and 92(14) of the B.N.A. Act as they apply to all the Provinces, and declared "...it appears to vest in the provincial Attorney General all the powers which that officer held by law at the time of Confederation and *to make such powers subject to change only by the*

16

provincial Legislatures".[43] Whether this view as to the apparent entrenching effect of section 135 will prevail will not become evident until the next chapter, following *Hauser*, of the saga involving the federal and provincial Attorneys General and their prosecutorial powers is written by the Supreme Court of Canada.

Without recourse to the confirmatory provision of the Law Officers' powers in the B.N.A. Act, s.135, available to Ontario and Quebec, the new provinces resorted to legislation of their own making. Manitoba led the way in 1885, placing on its statute book a comprehensive calendar of the Attorney General duties.[44] This enactment set forth the Law Officer's functions as follows:

"(a) He shall be the official legal adviser of the Lieutenant Governor and the legal member of the Executive Council;
(b) He shall see that the administration of public affairs is in accordance with law;
(c) He shall have the superintendence of all matters connected with the administration of justice in the Province of Manitoba, not within the jurisdiction of the Government of Canada;
(d) He shall advise upon the Legislative Acts and proceedings of the Legislature of Manitoba, and generally advise the Crown upon all matters of the law referred to him by the Crown;
(e) He shall be entrusted with the powers and charged with the duties which belong to the office of the Attorney General and Solicitor General of England by law or usage, so far as the same powers and duties are applicable to the province of Manitoba, and also with the powers and duties which, by the laws of Canada and the Province of Manitoba to be administered and carried into effect by the Government of the Province of Manitoba, belong to the office of the Attorney General and Solicitor General;
(f) He shall advise the heads of the several departments of the Government upon all matters of law connected with such departments;
(g) He shall be charged with the settlement of all instruments issued under the Great Seal of the Province of Manitoba;
(h) He shall have the superintendence of asylums, prisons, houses of correction and other places of confinement within the Province of Manitoba;
(i) He shall have the regulation and conduct of all litigation for or against the Crown of any public department in respect of any subjects within the authority or jurisdiction of the Legislature of Manitoba;
(j) He shall be charged, generally, with such duties as may be at any time assigned by law or by the Lieutenant Governor-in-Council to the Attorney General of Manitoba."

The similarity between the above terms and those contained in the statute of 1868 pertaining to the functions of the Minister of Justice and Attorney General of Canada will be readily apparent to the reader. Almost the identical language is used to enumerate the functions of the Attorney General of Manitoba in that province's Revised Statutes of 1970.[45]

The model set by the Manitoba statute of 1885 was followed by British Columbia in 1899[46] when it established, for the first time, the Department of the Attorney General, presided over by the Attorney General of British

Columbia. That colony's legislature had earlier, in 1871, in anticipation of its entry into Confederation, made provision for an executive council including the Attorney General. The 1871 measure provided that "all rights, powers, duties, functions, responsibilities or authorities" vested, at the passing of the Act, in the major officers, including the Attorney General, by any proclamation, law, act or ordinance then in force, should continue to be vested in or imposed on these officers.[47]

Nova Scotia in 1900,[48] then Saskatchewan[49] and Alberta[50] in 1906, all copied the pattern set by Manitoba, in each case including within their appropriate statutes a clause stating that the provincial Attorney General "shall have the functions and powers which belong to the office of Attorney General of England by law or usage so far as the same are applicable to the province". Whereas, however, the Nova Scotia Public Service Act, 1906, added also a clause which included "the functions and powers which previous to the coming into force of the B.N.A. Act, 1867, belonged to the office of Attorney General in the province of Nova Scotia and which under the provision of that Act are within the scope of the powers of the Government of the province" the newer provinces referred to the functions and powers which, up to the Union, had belonged to the offices of Attorney General and Solicitor General in the late Province of Canada.

It is impossible to discern, in this account of legislative action by the provinces, any systematic concern for regulating the prerogative powers of the Attorney General and Solicitor General. Astonishing as it may seem in retrospect, only within the past decade has Ontario seen fit to give statutory form to the functions, duties and powers of the provincial Attorney General. Prior to its recent legislation, the authority of the Attorney General of Ontario was derived from the British North America Act, 1867, section 63 (to which reference has already been made) as well as sections 134 and 135, and, in particular, from its own Executive Council Act, 1877, which enabled the Governor-in-Council "from time to time, to prescribe the duties of those officers (i.e. members of the Executive Council) and of the several departments over which they shall preside or to which they shall belong and of the officers and clerks thereof".[51] In a move that savoured somewhat of not wishing to be seen in an inferior light, the Legislature of Ontario in 1969[52] reconstituted the former Department of the Attorney General as the provincial Department of Justice, in line with the same move taken by the Quebec Government in 1965.[53] Henceforth, it was proclaimed, the Attorney General of Ontario was to be known as the Minister of Justice and continue *ex-officio* to be the province's Attorney General.[54]

So that the reader can readily discern how closely the formulation of the Minister of Justice's functions adheres to that set forth in the statutes of the other provinces, it may be helpful to cite in full the relevant section of the Ontario Department of Justice Act 1968-69. The Minister of Justice and Attorney General of Ontario, it declares:[55]

"(a) is the Law Officer of the Executive Council;
(b) shall see that the administration of public affairs is in accordance with the law;

18

(c) shall superintend all matters connected with the administration of justice in Ontario;

(d) shall perform the duties and have the powers that belong to the Attorney General and Solicitor General of England by law or usage, so far as those duties and powers are applicable to Ontario, also shall perform the duties and have the powers that, up to the time of the British North America Act, 1867 came into effect, belonged to the offices of the Attorney General and Solicitor General in the provinces of Canada and Upper Canada and which, under the provisions of that Act, are within the scope of the powers of the Legislature;

(e) shall advise the Government upon all matters of law connected with legislative enactments and upon all matters of law referred to him by the Government;

(f) shall advise the Government upon all matters of a legislative nature and superintend all Government measures of a legislative nature;

(g) shall advise the heads of the departments and agencies of Government upon all matters of law connected with such departments and agencies;

(h) shall conduct and regulate all litigation for and against the Crown or any department or agency of Government in respect of any subject within the authority or jurisdiction of the Legislature;

(i) shall superintend all matters connected with judicial, registry and land titles offices;

(j) shall perform such other functions as are assigned to him by the Legislature or by the Lieutenant Governor in Council.''

Within less time than it took the general public or the legal profession in Ontario to adjust to the change in the title of the Ministry responsible for the administration of justice in the province, the Government in 1972 quietly performed a *volte face* and reverted to the old concepts of Attorney General and Ministry of the Attorney General.[56] All this was done in the cause of government reorganisation. The Ontario statute, *inter alia*, removed the Minister of Justice from the list of members of the Executive Council and, in his place, created the new office of Provincial Secretary for Justice with ill defined duties of a coordinating nature that embrace, but are not restricted to, the Ministry of the Attorney General and the new Ministry of the Solicitor General of Ontario. Having quickly discarded the Quebec model of a provincial Ministry of Justice it is rather ironic to record Ontario's ready assimilation of another new idea, this time pioneered by the Federal Government in 1966 when it converted the office of Solicitor General of Canada into a ministerial portfolio responsible for a full Department by the same name. Ontario's creation in 1972[57] of a provincial Department of the Solicitor General has been followed by Alberta in 1973,[58] in both instances with functions that primarily involve the supervision of the police forces in the province. Before examining the provincial legislation in these two provinces we must turn to the office of the Solicitor General of Canada which is of major interest to the present Commission of Inquiry.

4. Antecedents of the office of Solicitor General of Canada

Since the functions and responsibilities of the Solicitor General of Canada are central to the Commission of Inquiry's terms of reference it is important that we trace the emergence of this office on the constitutional scene in Canada and note carefully the departures that have recently occurred in designating the scope of the minister's principal duties. Originally patterned on the model associated with the Solicitor General of England, all the available evidence points to the Solicitor General in both Upper and Lower Canada being regarded as the *secondarius attornatus*, the lieutenant who was expected to assist the Attorney General in the discharge of his duties as the senior Law Officer of the Crown.[59] Interestingly, the appointment of Canada's first Solicitor General in 1782 by Governor Haldimand owed nothing to any anxiety about the burdensome duties of the Attorney General. There had been no cries of complaint on that score from the incumbent, James Monk, only the endless supplications for the payment of fees due to him. It is noteworthy that the office of Solicitor General nowhere appears in the establishment of government offices prepared at the time of the Quebec Act, 1774, nor in the list of appointments which were sent to Governor Haldimand in April, 1775 by the Secretary of State for the Colonies. In appointing Jenkin Williams, a Welshman and former clerk of the Executive Council, as Quebec's first Solicitor General, Haldimand seems to have been prompted more by a determination to ensure a more dependable and less politically active government lawyer, with an added desire to divert away from Attorney General Monk some of the lucrative sources of income associated with the office.[60]

This is not the time to pursue the problems attendant on the mode of remunerating the Law Officers for their services as the government's lawyers, a subject that seems to have repeatedly occupied the attention of the early Governors of the colony, as well as their Whitehall masters. We have already noted the unsuccessful move advanced by Sir John A. Macdonald, when in opposition, to reintroduce the defunct office of Solicitor General as the best means of alleviating the increasing burdens of office that were said to have accompanied the expansion of work in the federal Department of Justice.[61] Due to the dissolution of Parliament in December 1878, the Government's Bill which proposed the elevation of the office of Attorney General of Canada to a Cabinet portfolio, died before it could be successfully navigated through the Senate. On his return to power, though not immediately, Sir John A. Macdonald did precisely what he had advocated several years earlier from the Opposition Bench.

When the Parliament of Canada approved the creation of the Office of Solicitor General of Canada in 1886 we find the same uncertainty as to the precise functions of the office that led the legislators of Upper Canada to view the office as a dispensable fifth wheel within government. The terms of the statute of 1886 were brief. "The Governor-in-Council" it declared "may appoint an officer called the Solicitor General of Canada who shall assist the Minister of Justice in the counsel work of the Department of Justice and shall be charged with such other duties as are at any time assigned to him by the Governor-in-Council".[62] It will be noted that appointments to the resuscitated office were to be by Order-in-Council and not, as in the case of the Minister of Justice and other ministers of the Crown, by virtue of the Great Seal of Canada. The above terms of reference remained practically unchanged for the next 80 years.

It appears that the office was created in order to avoid the payment of large fees to outside counsel in connection with the business of the Department of Justice.[63] When Sir Charles Fitzpatrick was Solicitor General from 1896 to 1902 he took briefs for the Crown in the Supreme Court and the Exchequer Court. By the time that Arthur Meighen was first appointed Solicitor General of Canada in 1913, the Deputy Minister of Justice was invariably the leading counsel for the Crown in cases that reached the Supreme Court or the Judicial Committee of the Privy Council. In 1917 Arthur Meighen became the first Solicitor General of Canada to enter the Cabinet and the Privy Council as a fully fledged member in his own right. Previously he had been, as Solicitor General, a member of the Ministry only and not of the Cabinet.[64] The example set with respect to Meighen has been generally, though not universally, followed ever since.[65]

This change in ministerial status did nothing to enhance the practical responsibilities of the Solicitor General which, in the main, were concerned with advising the Governor General on the exercise of the prerogative of mercy in all cases except those involving the death penalty. This covered a motley group consisting of applications under the old Ticket-of-Leave Act, the remission of fines and forfeitures, temporary releases from prison for compassionate reasons, and applications for ordinary pardons. In capital cases, where commutation of the death sentence might be involved, the Minister of Justice, and not the Solicitor General, was responsible for advising the Governor General. This was certainly so at the turn of the century when attention to the allocation of responsibility for capital cases in the Department of Justice surfaced in the House of Commons in a strange way. The activities of the then Solicitor General, in conducting a large private practice simultaneously with his official duties, occasioned a sharp exchange in the Commons in 1899,[66] the holder of the office acknowledging that the question as to whether he should practise in the criminal courts or not was an open question. To allay the fears that were expressed to the effect that the Solicitor General might be placed in a conflict of interest situation, having to review a petition for clemency on the part of an accused convicted of murder and for whom the Solicitor General had acted as defence counsel, Sir Charles Fitzpatrick explained that "from the time the petition is received in the [Department of Justice] until it reaches [the Executive] Council the papers never reach me and I never have anything to do with them".[67] At that time, the recommendation as to a possible commutation of the death penalty was exclusively within the hands of the Minister of Justice. The change whereby the Solicitor General became responsible for both the review of the petitioner's file in a capital case and also the formal recommendation to the Executive Council appears to have taken place around 1952, if reliance is to be placed on an exchange in the Commons between Mr. Diefenbaker and the then Minister of Justice, Mr. Stuart Garson.[68]

When it is learned that not until 1959 was the Solicitor General empowered to act as Minister of Justice in the absence of the Minister,[69] it should come as no surprise to read critical comments being expressed in the House of Commons that the Solicitor General of Canada was nothing more than a highly paid parliamentary secretary and urging that some of the duties associated with the Department of Justice should be transferred totally to the jurisdiction of the Solicitor General thereby placing that office "in a much more decent light than it is at the moment".[70] A private member's Bill to that effect was unsuccessfully introduced in May 1961, being dismissed by the Government's spokesman as "frivolous and ridiculous".[71] The time for change, however, was fast approaching.

5. Transformation of the office of Solicitor General of Canada to full departmental status

The year 1966 marks the transformation of the office of Solicitor General of Canada from that of relative obscurity to its present day position of high political visibility. Although the Glassco Royal Commission on Government Organization, which reported in 1962, had specific recommendations to make with regard to the need to integrate the legal services throughout the federal sphere within the Department of Justice,[72] it made no reference to the pressing need to dissociate any major responsibilities from the Minister of Justice and Attorney General of Canada. The conclusion is inescapable that neither the government nor the Glassco Commission at that time perceived any serious problems that called for reorganisation of the duties set out in the original statute of 1868.

Yet, within the short space of three years the Pearson Government introduced, first, an Order-in-Council[73] and later, close on its heels, the Government Organization Act, 1966, effecting the transfer to the Solicitor General of Canada of the powers, duties and functions previously exercisable by the Minister of Justice and Attorney General of Canada with respect to:

(a) reformatories, prisons and penitentiaries,
(b) parole and remissions and
(c) the Royal Canadian Mounted Police.[74]

The introduction of this legislation was in accordance with the Canadian constitutional convention that the creation of a new department of government required Parliamentary approval and should not be effectuated by prerogative action. In traditional language the Government Organisation Act, 1966, s.2 provides:

"(1) There shall be a department of the Government of Canada called the Department of the Solicitor General over which the Solicitor General of Canada appointed by Commission under the Great Seal of Canada shall preside.

(2) The Solicitor General of Canada holds office during pleasure and has the management and direction of the Department of the Solicitor General."

Looking at the political scene in 1965 why, it may be asked, did the Pearson Government introduce measures that effectively truncated parts of the major responsibilities associated with the Department of Justice during the greater part of its existence? A review of the statements made at the time in the House of Commons by the Prime Minister, the Minister of Justice and the Solicitor General, who was about to become the minister in charge of the newly created Department, provides an interesting comparison in emphasis.

Speaking in the Committee of Supply on March 7, 1966, in connection with the estimates of the Department of Justice, the Prime Minister said:

> "We hope to introduce legislation shortly which will establish, among other things, the department of the Solicitor General under a minister who will have responsibility for the R.C.M.P. and for security matters. This will be a responsibility to which he will be able to give considerable time, because this increasingly important aspect of the work of the Department of Justice will then become the responsibility of a separate minister. The new minister will be able to give much closer attention to these difficult problems than has been possible in the past. A high priority function of the new department will be to examine in detail the problems of espionage and subversive activities, and to determine how best to deal with them."[75]

These general observations must be placed in the context of the prevailing political circumstances. The Government had been assailed for its handling of the *Spencer case*. Having first appointed Mr. Justice Dalton Wells of the Ontario High Court to conduct an inquiry into that particular case, the Pearson Government later, somewhat reluctantly, established the Mackenzie Royal Commission "to examine the operations of Canada's security procedures with a view to ascertaining, firstly, whether they were adequate for the protection of the state against subversive action and, secondly, whether they sufficiently protect the rights of private individuals in any investigations which are made under existing procedures".[76] The Prime Minister justified the setting up of the Mackenzie Commission as being designed, in part, "to assist the Solicitor General in his particular and new responsibility".[77] In this regard, it is fair to conclude that the government's objectives and the approaches adopted to further these goals were clearly perceived and in fact fulfilled. It is no reflection on the work of the Mackenzie Commission that circumstances have later developed requiring the setting up of the present Commission of Inquiry to go over much of the same ground.

The same confidence cannot be generated in seeking to explain the government's reorganisation of the responsibilities for the administration of justice in the area of federal jurisdiction. In his speech introducing a resolution in the House of Commons that heralded the major restructuring of the federal government, Mr. Pearson spoke of the enormous increase in the burdens of the Law Officers and the government's legal advisers. This, the Prime Minister declaimed, called for a radical reform of the Crown's law offices. "On the one hand" he continued "the Department of Justice and the office of the Attorney General of Canada will be returned to the full time discharge of their traditional functions in the drafting of legislation and documents; the conduct of litigation and prosecutions... The R.C.M.P., criminal investigations, detentions, paroles and pardons, on the other hand, will be the full time responsibility of the Solicitor General in a department which, like the Home Office in Britain, will be separate and distinct from that of the Attorney General".[78] No elaboration of the reasons underlying this separation of functions in the constitutional government of Britain was advanced by the Prime Minister.

At the Committee stage of the Government Organisation Bill the Solicitor General, Mr. Larry Pennell, appears to have grasped the significance of the division of responsibilities in England and used it to refute the arguments of the Opposition who were predicting calamitous consequences from the emasculation of the Department of Justice. Referring specifically to the removal of the Royal Canadian Mounted Police from the jurisdiction of the Department of Justice, the Solicitor General declared: "Under the new bill there will now be a separation of the investigative functions of the police from the process of prosecution in the courts. It seems to me that to vest the authority for the investigative functions of the government in the same person who is going to conduct the criminal process is foreign to the spirit of justice."[79] Mr. Pennell further stated: "Under the proposals set forth in this bill the R.C.M.P. will carry out its investigations under the authority of the Solicitor General. But... the decision whether or not the facts disclosed by the investigation merit the commencement of a criminal prosecution will continue to be taken by the Minister of Justice in his capacity as Attorney General. Thus two sets of minds and two sets of responsibilities will be involved. It is my hope and belief that the efficiency of the criminal law process will be improved as a result... I would point out that the separation of the police and the Attorney General has for some time been and continues to be the practice in the United Kingdom. There the Home Secretary is the minister responsible for the police but the public enforcement of the criminal law in the courts remains the responsibility of the Attorney General."[80]

Apart from stressing that the Minister of Justice must and will remain solely responsible for determining whether, as the result of any investigation made by the R.C.M.P. or other agency charged with regulatory or investigative responsibilities under the law, there is a case for prosecution and for initiating the prosecution in all instances where this action lies within federal jurisdiction,[81] the Minister of Justice, Mr. Cardin, had nothing to say on the fundamental issue raised by his colleague, the Solicitor General. Instead, Mr. Cardin concentrated on the fact that "...in essence, [the proposed changes] are designed, to enable the Department of Justice to concentrate its full resources on those problems and tasks which, by the terms of the Department of Justice Act, 1868, were intended to fall within its purview. While the character of the department has not undergone any significant change since it came into being nearly a hundred years ago, the addition of other responsibilities — some closely related to its basic functions, others not so readily identifiable — has made it increasingly difficult for the Minister of Justice and Attorney General of Canada to perform his important duty as the principal law officer of the Crown."[82]

Earlier, I posed the question why did the Pearson Government insert into the Government Organisation Bill the provision establishing the new Department of the Solicitor General thereby changing the entire complexion of the Department of Justice? The passages quoted above from the prepared speeches of the leading spokesmen for the Government suggest a carefully orchestrated explanation of the government's moves. The fact remains, however, that no reference is to be found in the voluminous report of the Glassco Royal Commission on Government Organisation to the constitutional analysis that, according to the Prime Minister and his ministerial colleagues, led the

Government to propose some major surgery with respect to the functions of the Minister of Justice and Attorney General of Canada and which led, simultaneously, to the unexpected flowering of the ministerial responsibilities of the Solicitor General of Canada.

We are left with the inescapable suspicion that neither the Government nor the Prime Minister addressed their minds in 1966 to the ramifications of using the portfolio of the Solicitor General, an office exclusively rooted in the historical development of the Law Officers of the Crown, to describe the new Department that was to be responsible for the R.C.M.P., the federal penitentiaries, parole service and the National Parole Board. Some of these ramifications have surfaced in connection with the relationship that should exist between the Minister responsible for the Security Service of the R.C.M.P. and his Cabinet colleagues, in particular with the Prime Minister. Attention to this important question will be deferred to the concluding chapter of this study. In removing the country's major police and correctional agencies from the Department of Justice it might be expected that prior discussions as to the proposed reorganisation would have been entered into with the senior officials in the Department. On the contrary, there is good reason to believe that such discussions as took place were perfunctory and consisted of little more than the disclosure of a *fait accompli*. If this description of the events preceding the introduction of the Government Organisation Bill in 1966 seems farfetched and unreal, it is well to recall once more that nowhere in its final report did the Glassco Royal Commission either diagnose the so-called problems associated with the Department of Justice or advocate the drastic changes that led to the creation of the new Department of the Solicitor General.

6. The separation of policing and prosecutorial functions in terms of ministerial responsibility — the lessons of the Dorion Inquiry

All the reasons advanced by the Prime Minister and his law ministers may seem, from the present vantage point, to be rational and persuasive. Their accuracy, however, as the definitive explanation of the reasons underlying the organisation that took place in 1965 is open to doubt. One vital consideration appears not to have been publicly referred to and yet it is inconceivable that it should not have been prominent in the Cabinet discussions that preceded the introduction of the pertinent Order-in-Council. I refer to the findings of the Special Public Inquiry, presided over by Frederic Dorion, Chief Justice of Quebec,[83] which investigated allegations arising out of what became known as the *Rivard case*. Questions had been raised in the House of Commons in November 1964, the gist of which involved allegations that the Executive Assistant and the Special Assistant to the Minister of Justice, together with the Parliamentary Secretary to the Prime Minister, had exerted improper pressures upon counsel who was representing the United States Government in extradition proceedings against Rivard in connection with narcotics trafficking.

The Dorion Inquiry was set up to inquire into the truth of these allegations and, in particular, to inquire into the manner in which the Royal Canadian Mounted Police and the Minister of Justice, Mr. Guy Favreau, had dealt with the allegations when they were brought to their attention. The evidence tendered before the Commission established that Mr. Favreau had reached his decision not to prosecute on the basis of his reading the R.C.M.P. file and his personal questioning of the then Commissioner of the force, George B. McClellan.[84] Chief Justice Dorion, in acknowledging that the Minister, acting in his capacity as Attorney General of Canada, had full discretion to decide whether criminal proceedings should be instituted against the government officials concerned, concluded that Mr. Favreau had attached too great importance to the opinions expressed by the Commissioner of the R.C.M.P. In the view of the Commission of Inquiry, the Attorney General, before reaching his final decision, should have referred the file to the legal advisers of the Department of Justice, adding that "the very circumstances of this case should have led him to refrain from expressing any view at all, since his decision was to be of a quasi-judicial nature."[85] Chief Justice Dorion, in his final conclusions, properly drew attention to the fact that, apart from his duties as Minister of Justice, Mr. Favreau held several political and parliamentary offices that absorbed a great deal of his time and energy and prevented him from giving the R.C.M.P. file all the attention that it required. Nevertheless, the Chief Justice concluded, "the Minister of Justice, before reaching a decision, should

29

have submitted the case to the legal advisers within his Department with instructions to complete the search for facts if necessary and secured their views upon the possible perpetration of a criminal offence by one or several of the persons involved".[86] This unequivocal criticism of the Minister of Justice's handling of his ministerial duties led Mr. Favreau to tender his resignation to the Prime Minister and it was reluctantly accepted.

Despite the careful distinction that was drawn by counsel for the Government, in his closing address to the Commission of Inquiry, between the functions of the Minister of Justice and those of the Attorney General of Canada,[87] it is by no means evident from the report that Chief Justice Dorion fully appreciated that the above separation of functions was derived from the well established distinction that prevails in English constitutional practice between the investigative functions of the police and the prosecutorial discretion exercisable by the Attorney General or his agents. This separation of functions, it is suggested, was not breached by the Minister's failure to consult the full time legal staff in the Department of Justice. Rather, it was violated by Mr. Favreau's failure to comprehend that he had certain functions to perform, *qua* Minister of Justice, with respect to the R.C.M.P.'s investigation of the allegations, and an entirely distinct role to play as Attorney General of Canada when the decision was whether or not to authorise criminal prosecutions.

In a public lecture on "Penal Reform and the Machinery of Criminal Justice in Canada" given shortly after the release of the Commission's Report, I adverted to this same fundamental distinction, saying:[88] "...as the Dorion Inquiry has revealed, there is inherent in the system of direct and personal supervision by the Minister of Justice over the federal police arm, the R.C.M.P., possible conflicts of duty which suggests the need to reexamine the constitutional relationship between the Commissioner of the Force and the Minister of Justice. This is particularly so where the issue involves the institution or withdrawal of criminal proceedings in the federal area of the criminal law.

"It may be helpful in this context also to compare the position under English law. In Britain, the Home Secretary occupies an almost identical position to our Minister of Justice so far as the Metropolitan London Police Force is concerned. In addition, the Home Secretary exercises supervision over all the country's police forces through the medium of Inspectors of Constabulary and the highly effective sanction of withholding exchequer grants from the local police authority. Significantly, however, since 1946 there has been a complete divorce of the Home Office from any control over criminal prosecutions, no matter what the offence charged...this responsibility rests with the Attorney General of England and, under him, the Director of Public Prosecutions. This division of functions, facilitated to some degree by the separate offices, has contributed greatly to the independence from political pressures which must be the goal of every State's administration of justice."

Turning to the Canadian system of government I pointed out that, at that time, "the portfolios of Minister of Justice and Attorney General are combined in all cases in the same person. This is so at the federal level, in the newly designated ministry within the province of Quebec, and in each of the other provinces where the one title of Attorney General encompasses all the diverse functions carried out in the Department concerned. If the principle of independence in the field of criminal prosecutions justifies the fundamental place that I accord to it in the machinery of justice, it is necessary to subject our existing governmental structure to careful reexamination''. In conformity with the same line of reasoning I also drew attention ''to what in theory constitutes a disturbing feature of the machinery of justice in every province. I refer to the combination in one Minister of the Crown, the Attorney General, of indirect but ultimate control over the personnel who maintain the three constituent branches of the administration of criminal law, namely the police forces that are responsible for the enforcement of the criminal law, the Crown Attorneys who prosecute criminal offences, and the magistracy who adjudicate upon the cases that concern the Crown and the individual offender. The history of other countries at least suggests the possible damage that such a combination of power in the one department of government can create''.[89]

My lecture concluded with these words: ''Given the personal qualities of integrity, and a proper understanding of the fundamental need to keep distinct the operation of the separate organs and to ensure that those who fulfill these responsibilities are allowed to do their work free from any suggestion of improper influence from any quarter, the danger may never protrude itself into public notice. But should it do so, we may well find ourselves directing our attention to the existing machinery and asking the pertinent question, what steps might be taken to minimize the possibility of any conflict of interest arising within the department of government for which the Attorney General is constitutionally responsible. Should the state, in effect, be content to rely upon the personal qualities of the incumbent who occupies the office of the Attorney General, and likewise of his permanent staff? The alternative course of action, for which I believe the time is now opportune, is to heed the lessons of the Dorion Inquiry and, in an atmosphere devoid of party political prejudices, to subject the administration of criminal justice in the provinces to independent examination''.[90]

Whether these views had any effect on government thinking at the federal and provincial levels is not for me to say. In the public lecture I had urged translating the office of Solicitor General of Canada into a nonpolitical and permanent office in the Department of Justice with initial responsibility for all questions involving criminal prosecutions at the federal level. Ultimate responsibility and accountability would have remained with the Attorney General with concomitant powers of superintendence over the Solicitor General's functions, as is the constitutional position in many Commonwealth countries including Australia (both federally and in the States) and New Zealand. My suggestion was not adopted. Instead, as we have seen, a new Department of the Solicitor General was established, taking away those responsibilities for the Royal Canadian Mounted Police which the Minister of Justice, as such, formerly exercised and incorporating the same functions in the Solicitor General of Canada.

As briefly mentioned earlier, the Province of Ontario followed suit in 1972, transferring to a new Ministry of the Solicitor General supervisory duties, *inter alia*, for all the police forces in the province, in accordance with the provisions of the Ontario Police Act.[91] Responsibility for the entire machinery of prosecutions in Ontario was to remain vested in the province's Attorney General. When the Bill to establish the new Ministry came before the Legislature for second reading, the minister designate was hard pressed to point to any substantial reasons why the government had introduced the measure. Towards the end of an unimpressive debate, the Solicitor General designate adverted to the recommendations of the Committee on Government Productivity, composed of senior public servants and business executives, which had been appointed in 1969 to investigate the management of the Government of Ontario with a view to improving its efficiency and effectiveness.

In its 1971 Interim Report[92] the Committee advocated the setting up of a series of policy coordinating ministries, one of which was to be concerned with the justice field. With no analysis whatsoever of the reasons, that I have elaborated upon earlier, for separating police functions from the portfolio of the provincial Attorney General, the Committee simply recommended that a new Ministry for Public Protection, together with the existing Ministries of the Attorney General and Correctional Services, should constitute the Justice triumvirate in the proposed reorganisation of the Government of Ontario.[93] What was foreshadowed as a Ministry of Public Protection eventually emerged in 1972 as the new Ministry of the Solicitor General. In this way the office that had lapsed in 1867, having earlier been associated from 1791 onwards with the junior Law Officer of the Crown in Upper Canada, was reconstituted with duties and functions that bear no resemblance to its progenitor.

There can be little doubt that the Ontario move was influenced by the precedent set in 1966 by the federal Government though, as we have seen, the Department of the Solicitor General in Ottawa has taken under its wing responsibility for both the national police force and the federal correctional services. An important question, to which I shall return, is the extent to which the qualities of independence and non-partisanship that are traditionally associated with the Law Officers of the Crown in England and Wales, should continue to guide the occupants of the portfolio of Solicitor General, notwithstanding the fact that the present duties of the Solicitor General of Canada and the Solicitor General of Ontario include the direct supervision of police forces, a task completely foreign to their British counterpart.

There is some evidence that in the province of Quebec there exists an appreciation of the conflict of purposes inherent in the one minister having tripartite responsibilities for the police, prosecutors and the lower judiciary. In 1965, the Quebec Government, for political reasons that were scarcely concealed at the time, enacted legislation that conferred upon the Attorney General of the province the title of Minister of Justice, tailoring itself upon the federal model.[94] In redesignating the Department of the Attorney General as the Quebec Department of Justice no change, however, was made in the functions of the Solicitor General of Quebec. Unlike Ontario, the province of

Quebec had continued after Confederation to include the Solicitor General among the list of members of its executive council. Thus, in 1886 (c.98) we find an enactment dealing specifically with the Department of the Law Officers of the Crown, which was to be presided over jointly by the Attorney General and Solicitor General, both offices being described as the official legal members of the executive council.[95] This arrangement did not last long. In 1888 the duties of the Attorney General were separated from those of the junior Law Officer, the former alone being designated as the official legal adviser of the Lieutenant Governor and the legal member of the Council.[96] The same Act resulted in the demise of the office of Solicitor General of Quebec, a state of affairs that continued unchanged until 1964 when we find the office resurfacing in the Executive Power Act of that year with duties: "to act as attorney and counsel and to appear before the courts, at the request of the Attorney General, and in any legal matter or judicial proceeding the conduct of which belongs to the Attorney General" and "to fulfill such other functions and duties of a legal or juridical nature as the Lieutenant-Governor in Council may assign to him".[97] The resemblance, in this definition of functions, between the pre-1966 office of the Solicitor General of Canada and its modern Quebec counterpart is striking.

Throughout the period under review, the minister responsible for all police functions and for law and order generally in Quebec was the Attorney General. The case for separating ministerial responsibility for the police in Quebec from the Minister of Justice and Attorney General, to use the new title introduced in 1965, was canvassed in a Quebec Government White Paper entitled "The Police and the Citizens' Security" which was issued in July 1971.[98] It covers a wide range of subjects but of particular interest to us is the treatment of ministerial responsibility for the police in the province of Quebec. "Politically speaking" the White Paper declared: "the police must not be a state within a State. It must come under the jurisdiction of a minister who, in turn, is answerable to the National Assembly for it. The minister responsible for police matters, for the whole territory, must be in a position to assume powers and functions in order to be able to enforce law and order and to put up an efficient fight against crime. Therefore, it is imperative that such powers and functions in police operations, integration and organisation, be established and clearly defined."[99]

The White Paper's analysis of the problem is well informed and invokes the precedent set by the Federal Government in 1966, stating:[100] "Under present conditions, the Justice Minister and Attorney General is wholly responsible for law and order in the province of Quebec. There are two solutions as to whom should fall the responsibility over the police forces in general, either to the Justice Minister or to a minister specially entrusted with police matters. The first solution has the advantage of offering a specialised department and so to free the Justice Minister from contingencies due to police action, considering his natural role as an arbitrator. The second solution is called for, not only because it has the advantage of not linking justice with police action but also for practical reasons which are due to the extremely wide range of the Justice Department and the responsibilities of its incumbent. This

33

solution was adopted at the federal level where the Solicitor General has responsibility over the R.C.M.P. A like solution was also adopted in France and in England where responsibility over police matters rests either with the Home Secretary or with the Minister of the Interior, as the case may be.''

Specifically, the Quebec Justice Minister's White Paper recommended:

"(i)   That the Justice Minister and Attorney General assume responsibility over police matters until such time when the reforms advocated in the White Paper are implemented.

(ii) That there be set up a headquarters for police matters, under the authority of a deputy minister responsible for police matters, that will come under the Justice Minister until a separate department has been set up.

(iii) That the Deputy Minister in charge of the headquarters of police matters, *interalia*, to ensure cooperation and coordination among the police forces concerned in the fight against terrorism — set up a multidisciplinary section whose responsibility would be to look into the activities of revolutionary groups.''[101]

Despite the well argued presentation by Mr. Choquette, the then Minister of Justice, for the separation from his portfolio of responsibilities for the police the situation in Quebec has remained unchanged. To the best of my knowledge the case for reform has taken a low place in the legislative priorities of subsequent Governments in the province of Quebec.

7. Membership of the Cabinet by the Attorney General and the Solicitor General and its bearing on the application of ministerial responsibility — a brief historical survey

Before we turn to examine the application of the doctrine of ministerial responsibility to the special position occupied by the Attorney General of Canada and the Solicitor General of Canada, it is important that a major difference in constitutional practice be noted, as between Britain and the other Commonwealth countries, including Canada, with respect to membership within the Cabinet. Ever since 1928 the Attorney General of England and Wales has not been included among the members of the British Cabinet.[102] He is a Minister of the Crown and, together with the Solicitor General, the Lord Advocate and the Solicitor General of Scotland, takes his place among the list of Ministers who collectively represent the Government of the day. Some or all of the four Law Officers, as the occasion demands, which is increasingly frequent, may be summoned to attend meetings of the Cabinet or of Committees of the Cabinet for the purposes of tendering legal advice. In Canada, on the other hand, from the inception of Confederation the Attorney General of Canada, by virtue of the integration of this office with that of Minister of Justice, has consistently been a senior member of the Cabinet. Indeed, as stated earlier, the first Prime Minister of Canada, Sir John A. Macdonald, combined his responsibilities as First Minister from 1867 to 1873 with those of the Minister of Justice and Attorney General of Canada.

This was in no way an extraordinary precedent. Well into this century many instances occurred wherein the Premier of a provincial government also fulfilled the duties of Attorney General.[103] Such an eventuality was, and remains, unheard of in Britain. Even on the question of the Attorney General's inclusion within the ranks of Cabinet members, it is significant that no other country in the Commonwealth has seen fit to emulate the strongly held conviction among British constitutional lawyers and politicians alike that it is more appropriate that the Attorney General's independence, and *a fortiori* the Solicitor General, should not be blurred by their inclusion in the Cabinet, the body that may have to take decisions on policy after receiving legal advice from the Law Officers.

Writing in 1964 I endeavoured to rationalize this wholly unique relationship in terms of ministerial responsibility. It is an undoubted fact that only the most urbane surprise is normally expressed at the ability of successive Lord Chancellors to discharge their judicial functions with no suggestion of partiality that might be expected to manifest itself, however rarely, as a consequence of their membership of the Cabinet. "It is possible to argue" I wrote "that the constitutional objections to the Attorney General's membership of the Cabinet apply with equal force to his membership of the government. If the theory of collective responsibility still has any meaning in the machinery of government it may be claimed that, whether he is inside or outside the Cabinet, the first Law Officer is just as responsible as the rest of his ministerial colleagues for the rightness of the decisions that are reached. Of course, so far as the legal validity of decisions made by the Cabinet are concerned, and to which the Attorney is privy, the Law Officer's measure of responsibility naturally assumes different proportions. And it should not be assumed that when attending meetings of the Cabinet, though not as a member, the Attorney General would expect to confine himself to giving legal advice to his government colleagues. On the question of membership of the Cabinet itself, perhaps it is the outward manifestation of the Attorney General's dissociation from the inner council of the government that assumes the greatest importance in underlining his independence in the enforcement of the criminal law. By excluding the Attorney General from actual membership of the Cabinet the tradition may well have been enhanced that the subject of criminal prosecutions is outside the purview of the Cabinet's decision-making functions.''[104]

Deeply entrenched as this constitutional convention appears to be nowadays in the United Kingdom, the most thorough examination of its underlying theory took place outside of England in the early part of the nineteenth century. The setting for this debate was the Select Committee on Public Expenditure of the Legislative Assembly for the Province of Canada in 1850, preceded by an earlier review of the same question by a Select Committee of the Executive Council in 1846. At the root of the controversy was the old issue respecting the salaries and emoluments of the Law Officers and the precise nature of their relationship to the Government. Slowly but surely the campaign to limit, and later prohibit, the Attorney General and Solicitor General from engaging in private practice, whilst simultaneously receiving a salary or fees for conducting the legal business of government, was successfully accomplished many years before the same goal was attained in England and Wales.[105]

This was not so in the early 1800's. In its report to the House of Assembly of Upper Canada in March 1829, the Select Committee on Finance recommended that the Law Officers be paid salaries in lieu of fees for the legal business of government.[106] This theme persisted in the years immediately following. By 1833 the larger question of active political involvement by the Law Officers had surfaced and resulted in the summary dismissal by the Secretary of State for the Colonies of the Attorney General, Henry Boulton, and the Solicitor General, Richard Hagerman, for having voted in favour of the expulsion of W.L. Mackenzie from the Legislative Assembly, in opposition to the wishes of Her Majesty's Government in London.[107] Given the fact that appointment to both Law Officerships and their membership within the colony's Executive Council derived from the exercise of prerogative powers by the Colonial Secretary, their dismissal must have come as no surprise. Hagerman, it might be noted in passing, was later restored to favour and elevated to the position of Attorney General.[108]

In a despatch that underlines clearly the relationship perceived by the British Government towards the Law Officers of the Crown at the time, Goderich, the Secretary of State for the Colonies, wrote in 1833:[109] "... it appears to me not a little surprising that they [viz. Boulton and Hagerman] should have failed to perceive the extreme inconvenience of their continuing to fill the situations of Attorney General and Solicitor General while advocating, upon a question of great political and constitutional importance, sentiments directly at variance with those which Her Majesty's Government had expressed ... You will inform every member of either House, who holds an Office at the Pleasure of the Crown, that if he cannot conscientiously approve of the policy which Her Majesty's Ministers think it their duty to adopt, he must choose between his Seat in the Legislature and his Official Situations". In a postscript to his letter to the Governor of Upper Canada, Goderich added: "It does not appear to me by the Returns in my possession that Mr. Boulton and Mr. Hagerman are members of the Executive Council. If, however, they are so, the same reasons which render it impossible that they should continue to hold their situations as Law Officers of the Crown will also prevent their being members of the Council."

No despatch, it may be thought, could more obviously demonstrate the character of direct rule by the colonial power, and the ultimate source of power and authority at that time so far as the Canadian colonies were concerned. The important question that was to arise with the increased political activity on the part of those Canadians who occupied the positions of Attorney General and Solicitor General in the 1830's and 1840's, and the recognition by the Executive Council of its growing accountability to the Legislative Assembly, was the new constitutional relationship that was emerging between the Law Officers, the Executive Council and the Legislature as perceived by each estate.

Some of the initial signs of these relationships are contained in the Report of the Select Committee of the Legislature for the Province of Canada in 1850 and the previous Report of a Special Committee of the Executive Council in 1846. According to the earlier report:[110]

> "It is only since the Union that it has been understood to be requisite that the four Law Officers should have seats in Parliament, and take part in political affairs. Before that period the duties of their office required them:
>
> Firstly, — To conduct the Crown business before the Courts, so far as it might be in their power to do so.
>
> Secondly, — To advise the Departments of the Executive Government on points of Law whenever so commanded by the Governor, and to prepare Drafts of, or issue Fiats for, or examine and countersign, as the case might be, certain descriptions and (in Lower Canada more particularly) of public Instruments; to perform certain other ministerial functions in connexion with some of such Instruments; always also at the command of the Governor.
>
> The Solicitors General appear to have aided in the discharge of these Duties, only so far as the Attorneys General may have needed their aid, and in cases where the Governor may have specially directed their joint action.
>
> At the Union, the political duties of the Executive Councillor and Member of Parliament were superadded, and in these, until the change made in September 1844, the Solicitors General bore an equal share with the

Attorneys General. Since that change, the only political duties attached to the Solicitors General are such as follow from membership in the House of Assembly.

It was clearly not intended at the Union to allow the political or other duties of the Law Officers to withdraw them more than might be unavoidable, from the Courts of Law, and thereby throw that branch of their duties into the hands of Queen's Counsel.

In practice, however, the various official occupations of the Law Officers out of court were found more engrossing than was probably anticipated when they were all brought into the Executive Council. And hence arose the necessity for the change which has since removed the Solicitors General from this Body.

The opinion has been entertained, as the Committee are aware, that the same change ought to be made in the position of the Attorneys General also, that their presence in Council, by the demand which it makes on their time, and the constant importance which it attaches to their presence at the Seat of Government, is almost incompatible with their due discharge of their other functions, and more especially with those connected with the Courts of Law; that even apart from this consideration, there is an anomaly in their being called on, as they now are, first to advise Government on points of Law, and then to sit in Council, to discuss and decide on their own advice; and that in England, accordingly, none of the Law Officers have Seats in the Cabinet."

The Select Committee felt it imperative on them to observe that "they regard it as a point of the last importance that the duty of conducting the Crown business in the Courts of Law, should be discharged to the utmost possible extent by the highest Law Officers of the Crown, in person. It is, of course, necessary that the Attorneys General, so long as they shall be members of the Executive Council, should give such amount of attendance in Council at other times as the exigencies of the Public Service may require. But such attendance should on no account be suffered to prevent their personally taking part in the conduct of the Crown business in Court and more especially as regards the weightier class of cases."[111] By the time, however, that responsible government had been granted, as Professor J.E. Hodgetts has pointed out in his study *The Pioneer Public Service*: "the offices of Attorney General for Canada East and Canada West had become the centres where parliamentary strategy was planned and major administrative decisions were reached. It was no accident, then, that found the two premiers [of the dual ministries of that period] most frequently operating from these two offices". The outcome, according to Hodgetts, was that the Law Officers of the Crown provided "much of the central coordination which was expected of the Cabinet as a body. Not only were they responsible for directing political strategy in Parliament but also their legal abilities induced the other departments to appeal to them for rulings not always on points of law — which in turn came to be treated as rulings of the whole cabinet."[112]

That this state of affairs caused concern among some members of the Legislative Assembly in 1850 is apparent from the terms of reference which required the Select Committee on Public Expenditure to inquire "into the expediency of withdrawing the Attornies [sic] General [of Canada East and Canada West] from the Cabinet or Executive Council, and political business of the Government, except as members of this Honourable House, and of confining them exclusively to their official duties as the Law Officers of the Crown".[113] Testimony was called for from current and previous holders of the offices of Attorney General and Solicitor General. The proceedings reveal the same division of opinion on these contentious questions as that subsequently reflected among the members of the Select Committee when the time came to record their votes.

In enunciating the arguments against the inclusion of the Law Officers within the Executive Council, John Hillyard Cameron, a former Solicitor General declared:[114] "The Law Officers at present are obliged to give legal opinions, with a knowledge of their political consequence and be responsible for them. In the mode I propose, the legal opinions given would be totally irrespective of any political bearing and ought to be independent of the cases to which they may be applied." The contrary position was taken by Robert Baldwin, Attorney General for Canada West, who expressed himself as follows: "As respects dispensing with the office of Attorney General, as clothed with its present political character, I do not believe that in a community like ours it will be found practicable to do so with advantage to the public. There is, of course, no necessity arising out of the nature of the office for requiring that the holder of it should be the Head of the Provincial Administration, and I have no doubt that it will occasionally happen that the holders of other offices will occupy that position[115]... In most cases the leading man, of whatever party may be in the ascendant, will belong to the profession of the Law. In preparing, therefore, the list of an Administration for the consideration of the Representative of the Sovereign, such persons will naturally prefer the Office that keeps him, in form at least, connected with his Profession. Canada, is not, and for a period much longer than can be looked forward, for any practical purpose, cannot be in a situation in which an Administration can be advantageously formed wholly irrespective of what may be called the separate confidence of each section of the Province."[116]

When the motion "That it is expedient to withdraw the Attornies General from the political business of the (Executive) Government and to restrict them to their official duties as (principal) Law Officers of the Crown" was put to the Select Committee the motion was rejected by a vote of 33 to 5, Attorney General Baldwin (Canada West), and Attorney General LaFontaine and Solicitor General Drummond (Canada East) voting with the majority. Considerations of economy, rather than principle, appear to have prompted the Select Committee on Public Expenditure to recommend that "inasmuch as public prosecutions are not infrequently conducted by professional men specially retained, and as these Officers (viz., the Solicitors General) are not required to reside at the Seat of Government, the office may, with saving and without inconveniences to the Public Service, be dispensed with".[117] This particular recommendation was not adopted by the Legislative Assembly and it was to be many more years before the necessity of appointing a junior Law Officer of the Crown was once again to be assailed and temporarily resolved by placing the appointment in abeyance.

So far as I am aware, there has been no concerted move in Canada subsequent to the 1850 study to exclude the Attorney General, as such, from the membership of the federal or provincial Cabinets. In some of the other colonies, however, repeated attempts were made to make the office of Attorney General non-political.[118] New Zealand, for example, in its Attorney General's Act, 1866, provided that the commission of the Attorney was to be continued "during good behaviour", removal from office being dependent upon an address of both Houses of the General Assembly. In addition, express provision was made for the exclusion of the Attorney General from the Executive Council of the colony and of either House of the General Assembly. The experiment was short lived, for the New Zealand Attorney General's Act of 1876 enabled the Attorney General to be either a permanent and non-political officer or a member of the Cabinet at the discretion of the Governor-in-Council, the tenure of the office to be "during pleasure".[119] Despite the alternative choices provided for in the 1876 legislation, the office of Attorney General in New Zealand has ever since been held by a member of the legislature with a seat in the Cabinet, usually in combination with the portfolio of Minister of Justice. It is to be noted, however, that the Solicitor General in that country is the permanent head of a small and largely independent department of the public service called the Crown Office.[120]

8. The relationship in Britain between the Home Secretary and the Attorney General in matters of criminal prosecutions and pardons — comparisons with Canadian law and practice

At the time the Government Organisation Act, 1966 was being debated in the Canadian House of Commons, as we have observed earlier, both Prime Minister Pearson and the Law Ministers invoked the British constitutional model in support of the creation of a Department of the Solicitor General of Canada and the assignment to the office of Solicitor General of total responsibility for all the functions and duties associated with the Royal Canadian Mounted Police. Much play was made in those debates as to the separation of the roles inherent in the offices, respectively, of the Attorney General of England and Wales and the Home Secretary. Mr. Pearson spoke of the "course pioneered many years ago in the United Kingdom in the Home Office"[121] whilst the Solicitor General of Canada recalled that "It has always been thought in the United Kingdom that there ought to be an officer other than the Attorney General who is responsible for what they call preserving the Queen's peace within the realm, and that he should discharge the responsibility for the internal safety of the country, including security. It is on this basis that the Home Secretary has been responsible for the police since 1829."[122]

To any close student of British constitutional history it would be unfortunate if, in interpreting the respective roles and areas of ministerial responsibility of the British Home Secretary and the Attorney General, too much reliance was to be placed on the interpretation of these offices by the Canadian Prime Minister and the Canadian Solicitor General in 1966. We need to delve more carefully into the relationship between these two high Officers of State in the United Kingdom because of the parallels that continue to be drawn between, on the one hand, the policing and internal security functions of the Home Secretary and those of the Solicitor General of Canada and, on the other hand, the nature of the prosecutorial powers associated with the offices of the Attorney General of England and his counterpart the Attorney General of Canada.

Strict adherence to the constitutional principle that all decisions which pertain to the initiation or withdrawal of criminal prosecutions are matters for the Attorney General and him alone is now accepted by all political parties in the United Kingdom. The turning point in the resolution of this fundamental issue was the handling of the famous *Campbell case* in 1924 by the Ramsay Macdonald Cabinet. The full story of this episode, and the subsequent defeat of the first Labour Government, is documented in my study of *The Law Officers of the Crown* in 1964.[123] It would be erroneous, however, to conclude

41

that this understanding of the respective roles of the Attorney General and the Home Secretary was shared to the hilt by the Home Office before 1924 or for many years subsequent to the Campbell affair.

Particularly in the field of what might be described as political prosecutions, by which is meant prosecutions that involve considerations of policy relating to matters of internal security in the broadest sense of that term, we find the former Permanent Under Secretary of State for Home Affairs expressing the firm opinion in 1925 that a distinction had to be drawn between the legal aspects of a case and the question of policy that might be involved. As to the former, Sir Edward Troup wrote: "...the Home Secretary would almost always regard the opinion of the Law Officers as final".[124] Within the ambit of questions of policy Troup included the determination whether, in the existing circumstances, it would best serve the public interest to prosecute a man or to ignore the offence and avoid giving advertisement to the offenders, as to which the Permanent Under Secretary maintained "it is one which the Home Secretary must either himself decide or, if the matter be of first importance, bring before the Prime Minister or the Cabinet".[125] Precedents supporting this position show that, on a number of occasions both during and immediately following the First World War, both the government and notable occupants of the Attorney General's office participated in decisions that effectively transferred the ultimate responsibility for prosecutorial decisions from the Attorney General to the Home Secretary or, beyond him, to the Cabinet of the day.[126]

To understand these deviations from the modern conception of where ministerial control and accountability are said to reside it is necessary to refer to the relevant legislation, at the time, governing the areas of responsibility of the Attorney General and the Home Secretary in the enforcement of the criminal law. Thus, under the Prosecution of Offences Act, 1879, section 2, it was provided that "It shall be the duty of the Director of Public Prosecutions under the superintendence of the Attorney General to institute, undertake or carry on such criminal proceedings... as may be for the time being prescribed by regulations under this Act or may be directed in a special case by the Attorney General".[127] Among the cases prescribed by the prevailing regulations of January 26, 1886, as incumbent upon the Director to institute was the category "where an order in that behalf is given to the Director by the Secretary of State [for Home Affairs] or by the Attorney General".[128] No further elaboration was provided in the regulations delineating the specific areas within which the Home Secretary and the Attorney General were to be responsible for assuming the initiative or exercising the final decision whether or not to instruct the Director of Public Prosecutions to proceed.

Left in this indeterminate position, conflicting claims to exercise ultimate "jurisdiction" might have been expected to arise. All the evidence suggests the contrary and lends support for the view propounded in a memorandum to the Cabinet in 1924 by the then Home Secretary, Sir William Joynson-Hicks, that: "For many years it has been recognized by successive Home Secretaries and Attorneys General that as regards offences involving no question of public security or state interest the decision whether a prosecution in a particular case should be instituted or not was one entirely for the Director and the Attorney General, but that where a prosecution might involve any consideration of public security or any interest of state it was the bounden duty of the Attorney General or the Director before deciding upon a prosecution to ascertain the views of the Ministerial Department best qualified to pronounce upon the public interest involved — the Department in ordinary 'political' cases being the Home Office".[129]

It will be noticed that the Secretary of State was claiming no more than the existence of a duty on the part of the principal Law Officer "to ascertain the view of the Ministerial Department best qualified to pronounce upon the public interest involved". The cases referred to in *The Law Officers of the Crown* convey a very different impression as to the practical relationship between the Home Secretary and the Attorney General in the matter of criminal prosecutions. In those cases in which either Sir F.E. Smith or Sir Gordon Hewart was involved, there is no indication that the Attorney General was merely "ascertaining the views" of the executive, whether represented in the person of the Home Secretary or of the Cabinet as a whole. The impression, rather, is left of the first Law Officer of the Crown concerning himself primarily with the technicalities of the criminal law and abdicating the assessment of the policy considerations, which ultimately dictate the courses of action to be taken, completely to the executive.[130] Close cooperation there had to be in giving effect to the statutory provisions, but the *Campbell case* was to focus public and Parliamentary attention on "the very delicately adjusted relationship" between the executive and the Law Officers of the Crown.

The task of comprehending and defining the respective areas of authority exercisable by the Home Secretary and the Attorney General in the administration of criminal justice continued to engage the attention of Parliamentary Select Committees up to 1946. Central to this ambivalence was the responsibility for superintending the work and decisions of the Director of Public Prosecutions. Until 1946 the exact nature of this superintendence was somewhat uncertain, for although the Regulations of 1886 had stated explicitly that "the action of the Director of Public Prosecutions shall, in all matters, including the selections and instruction of counsel, be subject to the directions of the Attorney General", the same regulations made it mandatory for the Director to prosecute any case "when an order in that behalf is given to the Director by the Secretary of State...".[131] In the first few decades of this century the Home Secretary of the day considered it his prerogative to instruct both the Attorney General and the Director of Public Prosecutions on the necessity for prosecuting any offences involving public security or an interest of state. It is not known when the Home Office's new policy of desisting from any interference in the conduct of criminal prosecutions was instituted, though the reverberations of the *Campbell* case must have contributed to the decision. Certainly, as both the Director of Public Prosecutions and the Permanent Under-Secretary of State at the Home Office testified before the Select Committee on the Obscene Publications Bill in 1958,[132] the Home Secretary's power under the 1886 Regulations had been abandoned in practice long before 1946. It was removed altogether when the departmental regulations were revised in 1946, the constitutional position of the Director of Public Prosecutions now being clearly laid down as subject, in all matters including the nomination of counsel, to the directions of the Attorney General.[133] Where questions of the public interest are involved it would be foolhardy for the Attorney General to determine the question of prosecuting or not with no regard to the opinions of those ministers, including the Home Secretary, whose ministerial functions might impinge on the subject matter of the proposed prosecution.

The classic modern exposition of the Attorney General's constitutional position in England and Wales was set forth by Sir Hartley Shawcross, speaking in the House of Commons in 1954.[134] Rejecting at the outset the suggestion that suspected criminal offences must automatically be prosecuted, Shawcross reminded the House of the view expressed by Sir John Simon in 1925 that: "...there is no greater nonsense talked about the Attorney General's duty, then the suggestion that in all cases the Attorney General ought to decide to prosecute merely because he thinks there is what the lawyers call 'a case'. It is not true, and no one who has held that office supposes it is".[135] Under the tradition of English criminal law, Shawcross continued, the Attorney General and the Director of Public Prosecutions only intervene to direct a prosecution when they consider it in the public interest. In deciding whether or not to prosecute in a particular case, the Attorney General emphasised, "there is only one consideration which is altogether excluded, and that is the repercussion of a given decision upon my personal or my party's or the government's political fortunes; that is a consideration which never enters into account".[136]

Turning to the wider considerations involved when a prosecution may concern a question of public policy or national or international importance, Shawcross maintained that in such cases the Attorney General has to make up his mind not as a party politician, but must in a quasi-judicial way consider the effect of prosecution upon the administration of law and of government in the abstract. "I think the true doctrine is", Shawcross declared,[137] "that it is the duty of an Attorney General, in deciding whether or not to authorise the prosecution, to acquaint himself with all the relevant facts, including, for instance, the effect which the prosecution, successful or unsuccessful as the case may be, would have upon public morale and order, and with any other consideration affecting public policy. In order so to inform itself, he may, although I do not think he is obliged to, consult with any of his colleagues in the government, and indeed, as Lord Simon once said, he would in some cases be a fool if he did not. On the other hand, the assistance of his colleagues is confined to informing him of particular considerations which might affect his own decision, and does not consist, and must not consist, in telling him what that decision ought to be. The responsibility for the eventual decision rests with the Attorney General, and he is not to be put, and is not put, under pressure by his colleagues in the matter. Nor, of course, can the Attorney General shift his responsibility for making the decision on to the shoulders of his colleagues. If political considerations which in the broad sense that I have indicated affect government in the abstract arise, it is the Attorney General, applying his judicial mind, who has to be the sole judge of those considerations."

Shawcross's statement to the Commons in 1951 represents the same philosophy as that expounded by the then Prime Minister, Harold Macmillan, when he stated in 1959: "It is an established principle of government in this country, a tradition long supported by all political parties, that the decision as to whether any citizen should be prosecuted, or whether any prosecution should be discontinued, should be a matter, where a public as opposed to a private prosecution is concerned, for the prosecuting authorities to decide on the merits of the case without political or other pressure. It would be a most dangerous deviation from this sound principle if a prosecution were to be instituted or abandoned as a result of political pressure or popular clamour."[138]

Since writing my book *The Law Officers of the Crown* in 1964 there have been, as might be expected, many instances in which the decisions of the Attorney General have been the subject of intense questioning and criticism in the British House of Commons. I have referred to these in the course of a recent essay on "Politics and the integrity of criminal prosecutions: Watergate echoes beyond the shores of the United States."[138A] Each of the later precedents will be seen to sustain the well established constitutional doctrine set out above and, at the same time, to recognize the complementary principle that, after the termination of the particular criminal proceedings, including the decision not to proceed with a criminal charge, the Attorney General is publicly accountable for the exercise of his discretionary powers.[139] The extent to which a Law Officer of the Crown may feel disposed to inform the House of Commons of the grounds upon which he made his decision in individual cases will vary according to the particular circumstances. It is unfortunate that this aspect of the Attorney General's constitutional position has not received the attention it deserves by either parliamentarians or constitutional writers. Its importance to the maintenance of public confidence in the administration of justice, however, can hardly be denied and we shall later examine in more detail the experience of the Canadian House of Commons in holding the Attorney General of Canada accountable for his ministerial actions.

No account of the constitutional relationship between the Home Secretary and the Attorney General of England and Wales would be complete without a reference to the exercise of the prerogative of mercy. It is performed by the Sovereign on the sole advice of the Home Secretary. The document conveying the Sovereign's decision reflects the historic origins of this aspect of the Crown's prerogative, stating: "...Now know ye that We in consideration of some circumstances humbly presented unto Us, are Graciously pleased to extend Our Grace and Mercy unto the said (Offender)".[140] As an internal Home Office memorandum explains, over the centuries "The practice developed of using the Royal Prerogative for two main purposes — to temper justice with mercy and to correct manifest injustice. With the subsequent introduction of formal machinery for judicial consideration of appeals from the decisions of the criminal courts, the scope and need for prerogative intervention has been considerably reduced so as to become more recognizably of the nature of a 'long-stop'; and the essential purposes of the Prerogative powers today may now perhaps be described as to correct injustice which cannot be corrected by the normal processes of law, and to exercise clemency in circumstances which could not have been considered by the courts".[141] An earlier Home Office memorandum in 1874, in enunciating the guiding principles which governed the exercise of the prerogative of mercy, had stated, *inter alia*, "The Law Officers (are) consulted on points of law".[142] There is good reason to suppose that the same arrangements govern the relationship between the two Ministers at the present day. No suggestion has been heard that the Home Secretary is subject to direction by the Attorney General. On the contrary, it could be argued that the accepted dividing line separating the bailiwicks of the two portfolios contributes in significant fashion to strengthening the independent exercise of the prerogative powers entrusted, in their respective spheres of responsibility, to the Home Secretary and the Attorney General. Thus, the ultimate decision to proceed or not to proceed with a prosecution is in the hands of the Law Officers of the Crown. If, however, the ensuing prosecution, conviction and rejection of an appeal by the appellate courts, results in what is considered by the Home Secretary to be a miscarriage of justice, the Minister can rectify the situation by advising the Sovereign to grant an absolute or conditional pardon. This separation of jurisdictional responsibilities for the various stages of a criminal case enhances the sense of impartiality which should be brought to bear in making the discretionary determinations.

If the Attorney General is confined to the tendering of legal advice to the Home Secretary with respect to invoking the prerogative of mercy what, it might be asked, is the position of other Ministers and the Cabinet as a whole? There is no question at the present day as to the sole and exclusive responsibility vested in the Home Secretary to advise the Sovereign; in effect to reach the final decision himself. Even at the time, not so long ago, when the death penalty was in existence for crimes of murder under English law, the Home Secretary alone shouldered the burden of deciding whether to advise the Sovereign that the law should be allowed to take its course or that the death sentence should be commuted to life imprisonment.[143] This was not always so. Up until the succession to the throne of the young Queen Victoria in 1837 the decision as to carrying out the death penalty was the subject of discussion, but not decision, by a Committee of Privy Councillors, presided over by the Sovereign in person.[144] The final decision was made by the King as a personal act of the Crown's mercy and incorporated in a document bearing the Great Seal.[145] At the end of every monthly session of trials at the Old Bailey, the Recorder of London would attend before the Privy Council to discuss the fate of those convicted of offences carrying the death penalty.[146]

The roots of the modern constitutional practice whereby the Home Secretary alone is responsible for advising the Sovereign on the application of the prerogative of mercy date back to the appointment of Sir Robert Peel as Home Secretary in 1822. In a series of clashes with George IV, Peel, during his first tenure of the office of Secretary of State, effectively changed the practice whereby the King decided for himself whether or not he would invoke the Royal Prerogative.[147] There was a short period between 1830 to 1837, during which the advice to the Sovereign, though tendered by the Home Secretary, appears to have been the expression of a collective view by the Cabinet.[148] With the enactment of the Central Criminal Court Act, 1837,[149] and the disappearance of the monthly Recorder's Report, the so-called "Hanging" Cabinet of Privy Councillors[150] was rendered redundant and was never convened again.

An unsuccessful attempt to revive the pre-Victorian practice was made in 1864 by Lord Ellenborough who introduced a Bill in the House of Lords which would have required the Home Secretary to act with the assistance of a Committee of Privy Councillors.[151] Two years later, however, a Royal Commission on Capital Punishment was told by the incumbent Home Secretary, Sir George Grey, that the Home Office favoured restricting the responsibility for advising the Sovereign in capital cases to a single Minister, namely, the Secretary of State for Home Affairs.[152] This view has prevailed up to the present time, with the qualification that, in Scottish cases, it is the Secretary of State for Scotland who exercises the advisory responsibilities. So far as is publicly known, there has been only one modern instance in which the decision regarding the prerogative of mercy in capital cases has been the subject of debate and decision by the British Cabinet, as opposed to the Home Secretary acting alone. It occurred during the First World War and involved the Irish Nationalist, Sir Roger Casement, who had been convicted of treason following the Dublin Rising in 1916. The Cabinet, it is reported, deliberated on at least three occasions before finally resolving to let the law take its course and have Casement, the ring-leader, executed. Thirteen of his followers had previously suffered the extreme penalty.[153]

What of the position in Canada? How far are the English precedents explanatory of the doctrine of ministerial responsibility with regard to the prerogative of mercy? Historically, from the mid-1770s onwards, a different pattern from English law was emerging in the government of the distant colony, a pattern that is reflected also in the early history of colonial rule in Australia and New Zealand.[154] Theoretically, when direct rule from London was the order of the day and the Governor reported to, and received his instructions from, Whitehall, it could be said that the Secretary of State for the Colonies occupied an omnipotent position analogous to that of the Home Secretary in domestic matters. Certainly this was the case where offenders had been convicted of treason or murder, for these two crimes were consistently excluded from the normal arrangements that permitted the Governor of the Colony to administer the prerogative of mercy on behalf of the Sovereign. In practical terms, it came to be recognised that factors such as the distances involved, the slowness of communications with London, as well as the obvious advantages associated with first hand knowledge of the local conditions, necessitated a relaxation of the Colonial Secretary's control over the Crown's representative in the distant colonies. Confirmation of this amalgam of theory and practical exigencies is contained in the Royal Instructions issued in 1786 to Governor Carleton which stated:[155]

> "We do hereby give and grant unto you full Power and Authority where you shall see cause or shall Judge any Offender or Offenders in Criminal Matters ... fit Objects of Our Mercy to pardon all such Offenders ... Treason and Willful Murder only excepted in which cases you will likewise have power upon Extraordinary Occasions to Grant Reprieves to the Offenders until and to the Extent our Royal Pleasure may be known therein".

The same delegation of authority is to be seen in the warrants of successive Governors up to the appointment of Lord Colborne in Upper Canada in 1839,[156] by which time it was presumably felt to be unnecessary or undesirable to insert the exceptions for cases of treason and murder as requiring a reference back to the Secretary of State for his decision.

Further changes of an important kind were introduced in the Instructions prepared for the guidance of Sydenham when he assumed the office of Governor of Upper Canada in 1840. Here we find the first express recognition of a limited role being assigned to the Executive Council with respect to the making of decisions as to the pardoning of offenders, the Instructions declaring:[157]

> "Twenty-third. And Whereas We have by Our said Commission given and granted unto you full power and authority when you shall see cause or shall judge any Offender or Offenders in Criminal Matters, or for any Fines or Forfeitures due Unto Us, fit objects of Our Mercy, to pardon all such offenders and to remit all such Offences, Fines and Forfeitures. Now We do hereby require and enjoin you to call upon the Judge presiding at the trial of any offenders to make to you a written Report of the cases of all persons who may from time to time be condemned to suffer death by the Sentence of any Court within Our said Province, and such Reports of the said Judge shall by you be taken into consideration at the first meeting thereafter which may be conveniently held of Our said Executive Council, at which Meeting the said Judge shall be specially summoned to attend;[158] and you shall not pardon any such offender unless it shall appear to you expedient so to do upon receiving the advice of Our said Executive Council therein; but in all such cases you are to decide whether to extend or withhold a Pardon according to your own deliberate judgment whether the Members of Our said Executive Council concur therein or otherwise, entering nevertheless on the Minutes of said Council, a Minute of your reasons at length, in case you should decide any such question in opposition to the Judgment of the Majority of the Members thereof."

As will be seen, the Governor was empowered to override the advice of the Executive Council but the requirement necessitating a full statement of his reasons for departing from the judgment of a majority of the Council, to be formally entered in the Minutes and thus brought to the attention of the Colonial authorities in London, no doubt operated as a strong persuasive force in favour of decision by consensus. The same clause is repeated in the Instructions to Governor Head in 1854[159] and again to Monck in 1867,[160] by which time, in Britain as we have seen, the convention requiring the Sovereign to act strictly in accordance with the advice tendered by the Home Secretary had long since been established.

By 1878 all reference to the Governor General's power to override the will of the members of the Executive Council in matters of pardon had been removed, the Draft Instructions accompanying the Letters Patent issued to the Marquis of Lorne stating:[161]

> "We do hereby direct and enjoin that our said Governor General shall not pardon or reprieve any such offender without first receiving in capital cases, the advice of the Privy Council for our said Dominion, and in other cases the advice of one at least of his ministers ..."

Identical language was used in the Letters Patent prepared for the Governor Generalship of Viscount Alexander in 1947,[162] but the distinction drawn in the above Letters Patent between the sources of advice in capital cases and in all other cases was removed altogether in the statutory amendments to the prerogative sections introduced in the 1953-54 revision of the Criminal Code. The obligation of the Governor General to act in accordance with the advice of the Executive Council is enshrined in section 683 of the Code which reads as follows:

> "683. (1) Her Majesty may extend the royal mercy to a person who is sentenced to imprisonment under the authority of an Act of the Parliament of Canada, even if the person is imprisoned for failure to pay money to another person.
>
> (2) The Governor in Council may grant a free pardon or a conditional pardon to any person who has been convicted of an offence.
>
> (3) Where the Governor in Council grants a free pardon to a person, that person shall be deemed thereafter never to have committed the offence in respect of which the pardon is granted.
>
> (4) No free pardon or conditional pardon prevents or mitigates the punishment to which the person might otherwise be lawfully sentenced on a subsequent conviction for an offence other than that for which the pardon was granted".[163]

Although capital punishment has recently been abolished as part of Canadian law it is useful to recall that the same machinery and allocation of responsibilities were in vogue when the question arose of commuting the death sentence.[164] The disappearance of the death penalty from the Statute Book, however, has not occasioned any change in the contents of the current Letters Patent prepared for the Governor General, it also being noteworthy that the instructions relating to the advice that must be sought before pardoning an offender have remained unaltered from 1878 to the present day, the provisions in the Criminal Code, quoted above, notwithstanding.

In marked contrast to the constitutional practice in Britain, where the Home Secretary has been the supreme authority for the past 150 years, it is the Governor in Council, viz., the full Cabinet, that assumes legal responsibility in Canada for the exercise of the prerogative of mercy, albeit in the light of a thorough review of each case and the recommendation of the Solicitor General of Canada.[165] As we have seen earlier, the assumption of collective ministerial responsibility with respect to the pardoning of offenders derives from the early association of the Executive Council in advising the Governor when it was found to be impractical and inhumane, at least in capital cases, to defer the granting of a reprieve from execution until a ruling had been secured from the Colonial Secretary in far off London. No doubt, as time went on, the Law Officers in the Canadian colonies, who were responsible for making recommendations to the Governor and Council, were relieved to know that colonial constitutional practice did not impose sole responsibility upon their ministerial shoulders.

A further aspect of the laws governing the prerogative of pardon must be examined, if only to draw attention to some precedents set in the United States and Britain that raise important constitutional questions beyond the confines of those countries. The pardoning of Richard Nixon in 1974 by Gerald Ford, his immediate successor in the office of President of the United States, engendered widespread dismay and a storm of criticism. The main thrust of the criticism was directed against President Ford's decision to confer total immunity upon Nixon thus precluding any possibility of having his criminal guilt or innocence determined by the courts, in the same manner as befell Nixon's immediate associates including John Mitchell, the former Attorney General of the United States. According to the terms of the presidential pardon, conferred by virtue of Article II, Section 2 of the U.S. Constitution,[166] Richard Nixon was accorded "a full, free and absolute pardon — for all offences against the United States which he ... has committed or may have committed" during his years as the President.[167] In a submission to the House Judiciary Subcommittee on Criminal Justice on October 17, 1974, defending his decision, President Ford declared:

> "The pardon power entrusted to the President under the Constitution of the United States has a long history and rests on precedents going back centuries before our Constitution was drafted ... The Constitution does not limit the pardon power to cases of convicted offenders or even indicted offenders."[168]

There is no need here to pursue further the various arguments that have been canvassed as to the constitutionality of the Nixon pardon.[169] What is undeniable is that the Canadian law of pardon emanates from the same historical roots as those which sustain the relevant provisions in the United States Constitution.[170] Our immediate concern is to ascertain whether present-day Canadian law permits the pardoning of offenders before they stand trial.

The provisions of the Criminal Code, quoted earlier, seem crystal clear in denying the possibility of pre-trial pardon, section 683(2) stating:

> "The Governor in Council may grant a free pardon or a conditional pardon to any person *who has been convicted of an offence*" (my italics).[171]

There exists, however, in the Criminal Code a "catch-all" provision, section 686, which maintains that:

> "Nothing in this Act in any manner limits or affects Her Majesty's royal prerogative of mercy".[172]

Indeed, whenever any new legislative formulation of the ambit of the Crown's prerogative of mercy is embarked upon it is customary to find included a saving clause of the kind quoted above.[173] Given the express nature of the language used in section 683(2) it might be thought difficult to conceive of any convincing reasons that would justify a pardon that ran directly contrary to the conditions set by Parliament as to the granting of pardons. After all, the royal prerogative of mercy, under our system of a constitutional monarchy, can only be exercised in accordance with the advice of the responsible Ministers. Neither the Queen in England, nor the Governor General in Canada, would contemplate for one moment acting unilaterally in disregard of the recommendation of their political Minister(s), in whose hands the power of making the effective decision actually rests. What remains arguable is the possibility that section 683(2) is declaratory of one situation but does not purport to cover all situations in which a free or conditional pardon may be granted. In other words, the limitations set in section 683(2) are not conclusive as to the legal boundaries of the prerogative of mercy. Some qualified support for this position is to be found in the Instructions issued in 1878 to the Governor General of Canada under the Royal Sign Manual and Signet which contain the following provision:

> "We do further authorise and empower Our said Governor General as he shall see occasion, in Our name and on Our behalf, when any crime has been committed for which the offender may be tried within Our said Dominion, to grant a pardon to any accomplice, not being the actual perpetrator of such crime, who shall give such information as shall lead to the conviction of the principal offender ..."[174]

The above instruction was repeated in the Letters Patent, pertaining to the same office, which were issued in 1931 and 1947, and it is also contained in the instrument that currently sets forth the powers of the present Governor General of Canada.[175] Whereas, however, the power of pardoning an accomplice is exercisable "when any crime has been *committed* for which the (principal) offender may be tried", it is significant that markedly different language is used to define the conditions under which the principal offender or offenders may be pardoned. According to the same Letters Patent:

> "We do further authorise and empower our Governor General... to grant to any offender *convicted* of any such crime or offence in any Court, or before any Judge, Justice or Magistrate administering the laws of Canada, a pardon either free or subject to lawful conditions..."[176]

The above extracts from the prevailing Letters Patent governing the office of Governor General of Canada must be borne in mind when interpreting and applying the relevant provisions in the Criminal Code governing the prerogative of mercy.

The practice of granting a pardon to an accomplice who was prepared to turn Queen's Evidence was common in England during the nineteenth century but it has long since become obsolete in that country. Instead, any one of a variety of alternative procedures is adopted to achieve the same ends, including the offering of no evidence against the accomplice at either the preliminary hearing (resulting in his discharge) or the trial itself (resulting in his acquittal). The accomplice then gives evidence for the prosecution. In rare circumstances the Attorney General could enter a *nolle prosequi* with a view to the accomplice being called as a witness for the Crown, though a specific example of this use of the Law Officer's discretionary power cannot be recalled. In a situation where the reluctance of a witness to testify on behalf of the Crown did not stem from his being an accomplice but arose on the ground that he would incriminate himself, it was also known under English law in the last century for the crown to prepare a free pardon in advance, ready to be produced by prosecuting counsel. It appears that the last occasion when a free pardon was granted to a witness in these circumstances was in 1891.[177] The modern practice, as was dramatically illustrated in the criminal proceedings recently instituted against Jeremy Thorpe, the former Leader of the British Liberal Party, and his associates,[178] is for counsel representing the Director of Public Prosecutions to give a formal assurance to the parties involved that he does not propose to prosecute, and in the unlikely event of a private prosecution being launched he would exercise his statutory power to take over the prosecution and the case would then be handled in one of the ways described above.

Whichever way the question of a pardon to a principal offender *before conviction* is approached, the general understanding among British constitutional law authorities[179] is that the practice has fallen into disuse,[179A] the most important objection to any such practice is that it is out of harmony with modern views as to the propriety of granting dispensation before the normal process of the criminal law has run its course. There is all the more reason, therefore, to note the unusual precedent established in recent months, with little fanfare, when the British Government took action to ensure immunity from prosecution for Bishop Muzorewa, the Zimbabwe-Rhodesia Prime Minister. Muzorewa was on the point of visiting Britain for talks with Prime Minister Margaret Thatcher and her Cabinet colleagues when it became known that members of the Anti-Apartheid Movement, led by a Labour M.P., were proposing to have Bishop Muzorewa arrested and charged with treason and murder. The same problem, presumably, will arise when Ian Smith, the former Prime Minister of Rhodesia who was responsible for that country's unilateral declaration of independence in 1965, sets foot on British soil as a member of the Zimbabwe-Rhodesia delegation to the constitutional conference later this year.

To meet these contingencies the British Government has invoked its statutory powers under the Southern Rhodesia Act, 1965 which empowers Her Majesty by Order in Council to make such provision in respect to persons connected with that country "as appears to Her to be necessary or expedient in consequence of any unconstitutional action taken therein".[180] The action taken to ensure immunity from prosecution for Muzorewa, Smith and any other residents of Zimbabwe-Rhodesia who might otherwise face charges of treason is the enactment of the Southern Rhodesia (Immunity for Persons attending Meetings and Consultations) Order 1979.[181] Under its provisions a person to whom the Order in Council applies "shall, while within the United Kingdom, be entitled to the like immunity from suit and legal process and the like personal inviolability as is accorded, under the law in that behalf, to a diplomatic agent accredited to Her Majesty". The Order-in-Council was approved, laid before Parliament and brought into operation all on the same day, July 13, 1979. This extraordinary timetable scarcely permitted an opportunity for intelligent debate by the House of Commons with respect to its contents. In this regard the procedure of conferring prosecutorial immunity by Order-in-Council resembles the difficulties consistently encountered by the Opposition when seeking to question the Home Secretary as to the exercise of the prerogative of mercy.

So long as the death penalty remained on the statute book there existed a well recognised limitation on the right of an M.P. to question the Home Secretary whilst the execution was pending. Moreover, the uncommunicativeness of successive holders of that office in providing explanations, after the event, was rarely challenged successfully. This attitude and the support given to it by recent Speakers of the House of Commons has been trenchantly criticised.[182] It will be interesting to see what stance future Home Secretaries will adopt now that the emotional atmosphere of an impending execution has been removed from the forum in which the doctrine of ministerial accountability is invoked. Attorneys General, in recent times, have been relatively more forthcoming in providing an account of their reasons for instituting or discontinuing prosecutions, though the invariable practice has been to defer answers to Members' questions until after the criminal proceedings have been concluded.[183]

There can be no doubt as to the legality of the recent Order-in-Council, conferring what amounts, to all intents and purposes, to a free pardon with respect to possible crimes committed in the course of "unconstitutional action in Southern Rhodesia". After all, Parliament in 1965 saw fit to confer upon the Government delegated statutory power of a remarkably wide nature, within which the recent Order-in-Council is comfortably ensconced. It would be an altogether different situation if the prerogative rather than an Act of Parliament were to be invoked as the constitutional authority for extending a similar immunity from criminal prosecution. Should that eventuality ever occur it is to be hoped that the Members of Parliament would promptly remind Ministers of the Crown that such action evokes echoes of the Stuarts' dispensing power which was roundly condemned in the Bill of Rights in 1688.[184]

9. The Home Secretary's responsibilities for the police and security services in Britain — analogies with the Solicitor General of Canada

Leaving aside for the moment the separation of functions between the Attorney General and the Home Secretary in the British constitutional scene, the question remains — how appropriate is the analogy which was drawn by the Pearson Government in 1966, in support of its decision to create the Department of the Solicitor General, between the police and security service functions of the Home Secretary and the responsibilities in these same fields that were assigned to the Solicitor General of Canada under the terms of the Government Organisation Act? Since the enactment of the first Metropolitan Police Act in 1829 the organisation of the police in England and Wales has undergone many changes, the most notable of which has been the elimination in the past decade of the multiplicity of county, city and borough police forces and the redistribution of the nation's police manpower into regional units. In all this reorganisation the position of the Metropolitan London Police and its relationship to the Home Secretary has remained unchanged.

Much of the impetus for the reorganisation stemmed from the final report of the Royal Commission on the Police in 1962,[185] and is outside the scope of this paper. The 1962 report, however, did examine the relationship of police personnel to both the central authority, in the person of the Home Secretary, and to the local police authorities. In so doing the Royal Commission reaffirmed the "peculiarly personal nature of the constable's responsibility".[186] The courts in Britain have repeatedly reaffirmed the special constitutional status of its police.[187] In essence, this rejects the existence of a master and servant relationship between either the Home Office or local police authorities and the police officers of a particular force. For its part, the Royal Commission strongly supported the retention of the present legal status of the police on the grounds that in such matters as inquiries with regard to suspected offences, the arrest of persons and the decision to prosecute, what were loosely described as "quasi-judicial" decisions, "it is clearly in the public interest that a police officer should be answerable only to his superiors in the force and, to the extent that a matter may come before them, to the courts. His impartiality would be jeopardised, and public confidence in it shaken, if in this field he were to be made the servant of too local a body".[188]

The Commission experienced more difficulty in defining the status of the chief of police and his relations with the local or regional police authority. When dealing specifically with the kind of "quasi-judicial" matters referred to in the preceding paragraph, the Royal Commission entirely accepted the proposition that it is in the public interest that a chief constable "should be free from the conventional processes of democratic control and influence".[189] The problem areas, it was rightly deduced, were those which fell outside the enforcement of the law in particular cases and included such matters as the police chief's "general policies in regard to law enforcement over the area covered by his force, the disposition of the force, the concentration of police resources on any particular type of crime or area, the manner in which he handles political demonstrations or processions and allocates and instructs his men when preventing breaches of the peace arising from industrial disputes, the methods he employs in dealing with an outbreak of violence or of passive resistance to authority, his policy in enforcing traffic laws and in dealing with parked vehicles and so on".[190] With respect to these questions, it is important to note, the Commissioners rejected the prevailing doctrine that, as a consequence of his legal status, the chief of police is invested with an unfettered discretion, in which he is accountable to no one and subject to no one's orders as to the manner in which that discretion is exercised.[191]

Explaining the difference in its stance on the nature of police discretion in varying circumstances the British Royal Commission pointed to the situation that has always existed in the London Metropolitan Police. There, it was explained, "The Commissioner of Police acts under the general authority of the Home Secretary, and he is accountable to the Home Secretary for the way in which he uses his force".[192] Some elaboration of this general statement was provided by the Home Secretary when addressing the House of Commons in 1888, following the resignation of the then Commissioner of Police, in words that are equally applicable at the present time. "It was quite plain" said Henry Mathews, the Home Secretary, "that it was the intention of the Legislature to put the police force under the authority of the Secretary of State [for Home Affairs] and to hold him fully responsible, not for every detail of the management of the force, but in regard to the general policy of the police in the discharge of their duty..."[193] The practical effect of this principle is that the policies of the Commissioner of the Metropolitan London Police as regards the disposition of the force, the methods employed in preserving law and order and in law enforcement generally are frequently the subject of questions in the House of Commons to which the Home Secretary replies and, if necessary, he must defend the particular policy or procedures that are under scrutiny. Interestingly, the 1962 Commission drew attention to the view, entertained in some quarters, that the Home Secretary, in recent times, had gone farther in giving information to Parliament about the Metropolitan Police force than a strict interpretation of his responsibilities actually required.[194]

One of the central problems addressed by the Royal Commission was the case of bringing the chiefs of police throughout the country under some form of central control, in line with the special relationship that has historically existed between the Home Secretary and the head of the Metropolitan Police Force. As to this possibility, the Commission recognised the objections that such an arrangement would jeopardise the police chiefs' impartiality "since they would be placed within a hierarchy or chain of command leading ultimately to a Minister who was himself not required to be impartial".[195] In what represents a significant departure from the generally accepted application of the doctrine of ministerial responsibility to the Home Secretary, the Commissioners argued: "But the Law Officers of the Crown already hold offices which combine the characteristics of answerability to Parliament with the impartiality appropriate to the administration of justice. In the case of these Ministers, and, if the police were put under central control, in the case of Your Majesty's Secretaries of State [for Home Affairs and for Scotland] also, any evidence of partiality would be open to challenge in Parliament".[196] Scottish law, it should be explained, already empowers both a police authority and the Secretary of State for Scotland to call for reports on matters concerning "the policing of the area".[197]

There follows, in the Commission's final report, a detailed list of statutory provisions and non-statutory arrangements whereby direct and indirect controls are exercisable over chief constables.[198] Not the least of these controlling mechanisms relates to the powers of the Inspectors of Constabulary who are appointed by, and report directly to, the Home Secretary. In addition, there is the potentially potent sanction whereby the Secretary of State can withhold the exchequer grant amounting up to one half of the approved expenditure of a police authority. These elaborate arrangements, consistent with the present status of the police, represent an effective system of checks and counter checks with the minimum of directions and command. In short, it epitomises the British penchant for pragmatic development of its constitutional principles. The Royal Commission on the Police expressed the phenomenon in this way: "Why, then, do not the Secretaries of State take powers appropriate to the needs of the situation?... Perhaps it is because the purposes of Government have hitherto been adequately secured by persuasion and influence; perhaps because the powers which any Government may require are not always capable of precise definition; perhaps because any Government in this country would hesitate, on its own initiative, to seek from Parliament additional powers in relation to the police; above all, perhaps, because British experience in many fields of administration has shown that more can generally be achieved in the long run by persuasion than by compulsion".[199]

In its final recommendations, the 1962 Commission rejected the proposal that the British police forces should be brought under the direct central control of the Government with effective Parliamentary supervision,[200] preferring instead to recommend various steps that would assign a greater measure of statutory responsibility to the Home Secretary and the Home Office for the efficiency of the police. "It would be inappropriate" the Commissioners reported, "to assign to the Secretaries of State complete responsibility for the police service; it is implicit in our rejection of any arrangement under which the police should be placed under the control of the Government that Ministers cannot in our view be responsible for the acts of individual policemen or for the day-to-day enforcement of the law. Consequently the responsibility of the Secretaries of State should not extend beyond a general duty to ensure that the police operate efficiently and they should have no powers of direction. Thus we recognise a fundamental distinction between central responsibility for an efficient organisation, both central and local, and the responsibility of the police themselves, which is neither central nor local, for the enforcement of the law."[201]

Developing the same theme, the final report stated: "Within the scope of their general responsibility we distinguish four particular matters for which Ministers will be responsible. They will be responsible for ensuring the effective execution by police authorities of the authorities' duties; for the efficiency of each separate police force; for securing collaboration between groups of forces to promote the efficient policing of wider areas; and for the provision of ancillary services. In addition, the Home Secretary will continue to exercise his present powers in relation to the Metropolitan Police. Ministers are already equipped with powers to discharge certain of these responsibilities; but some of their present powers will need to be amended, and they will also require new powers".[202]

These measures have since been incorporated in the Police Act, 1964,[203] section 28 of which states in general terms that the Home Secretary "shall exercise his powers under this Act in such manner and to such extent as appears to him to be best calculated to promote the efficiency of the police". Henceforth, the Secretary of State will be able to be questioned in Parliament on the exercise or non-exercise of the powers and duties imposed on him by the 1964 enactment.[204] Gone is the fiction that because the Home Secretary did not control the police he could not be accountable to Parliament for matters falling within the scope of forces outside the Metropolitan London police. Time alone will tell how active the House of Commons proves to be in making a reality of the new dimensions of ministerial accountability for the police in Britain.

What then is the relationship between the British Security Service (often concealed under its mysterious title M.I. 5) and the Home Secretary, and how far is the Secretary of State accountable to Parliament for the acts or omissions of the Director General of the service and his agents? Under the British system the Security Service is responsible for intelligence and counter-intelligence in the general area of national security and, by the very nature of its broad mandate, has links with the Prime Minister, the Secretary of the Cabinet, the Foreign Office, the Ministry of Defence, the Special Branch of the Metropolitan London Police[205] and the other Special Branches that are an integral part of each of the other 42 police forces that are responsible for policing the rest of the country.[206] Normally it would be a difficult task to elaborate very much more on this question in view of the lack of published material dealing with this sensitive area of government. Fortunately for our purposes, no less a figure than Lord Denning, the Master of the Rolls, accepted the Government's commission in June 1963[207] "to examine, in the light of circumstances leading to the resignation of the former Secretary of State for War, Mr. J.D. Profumo, the operation of the Security Service and the adequacy of their cooperation with the Police in matters of security, to investigate any information or material which may come to his attention in this connection and to consider any evidence there may be for believing that national security has been, or may be endangered..."[208]

The national security aspects of the Profumo scandal, it will be recalled, arose out of the clandestine liaison with Christine Keeler on the part of both the Secretary of State for War and the Assistant Naval Attaché attached to the

Soviet Embassy in London. Lord Denning concluded that the senior officers of the Security Service were not to be blamed for their failure to warn the Prime Minister of his ministerial colleague's immoral escapades or of the links with a member of the Russian Embassy that might suggest a possible threat to national security. It was, according to Lord Denning, "an unprecedented situation for which the machinery of government did not cater".[209] The Master of the Rolls continued: "We are, I suggest rightly, so anxious that neither the police nor the Security Service should pry into private lives, that there is no machinery for reporting the moral misbehaviour of Ministers. Certainly, the police must not go out to seek information about it. Nor must the Security Service... When a Minister is guilty of moral misbehaviour and it gives rise to scandalous rumour, it is for him and his colleagues to deal with the rumour as best they can. It is their responsibility and no one else's".[210] Nevertheless, Lord Denning was mildly critical of the Prime Minister, the Law Officers and the Government Chief Whip for accepting, as conclusive, Profumo's denial that he had committed adultery.[211] Profumo's subsequent admission that he had lied to the House of Commons spelt the end of his political career, in addition to casting doubts upon the competence of the Macmillan Administration's handling of the entire affair.

Our interest with the Profumo Inquiry is less concerned with the salacious aspects of the case than in the account, which appears in Lord Denning's Report, as to the nature of ministerial accountability in Britain for the operations of the Security Service. First, we read a frank statement that the Security Service is not established by statute and its existence is not even recognised in the Official Secrets Act,[212] both observations being equally pertinent to the security service branch of the Royal Canadian Mounted Police[213] and the allied security agencies within the Ministry of National Defence and other federal Departments of Government in Canada. One major difference between the practice in the two countries relates to the powers exercisable by the Security Service. As the Master of the Rolls explains, in Britain members of the Security Service are regarded in the eyes of the law as "ordinary citizens with no powers greater than anyone else. They have no special powers of arrest such as the police have. No special powers of search are given to them".[214] What thus appears to be a legal vacuum, it is claimed, is made good by virtue of the close cooperation that exists between the Security Service and the country's police forces. The Master of the Rolls concluded: "If an arrest is to be made, it is done by the police. If a search warrant is sought, it is granted to a constable. The police alone are entrusted with executive power.[215] The degree of cooperation which is essential between the two services seems to be a further reason why the ministerial responsibility should be in one Minister, namely, the Home Secretary."[216]

Because of the widespread misapprehension that existed in political and government circles about the source of ministerial responsibility for the Security Service, Lord Denning elected to include in his report extracts from official documents that state the constitutional position in authoritative terms. Before 1952, he explained, the Prime Minister was responsible for security, in accordance with the theory that the purpose of the Security Service was "the defence of the realm".[217] According to an internal government study prepared in 1945 by Sir Findlater Stewart: "It follows that the Minister responsible for it as a service should be the Minister of Defence, or, if there is no Minister of Defence, the Prime Minister, as Chairman of the Committee of Imperial Defence. It has been argued that this would place an undue burden upon the Minister of Defence or the Prime Minister, and upon the staff of the Cabinet Secretariat. But from the very nature of the work, need for direction, except on the very broadest lines, can never arise above the level of Director General. That appointment is one of great responsibility, calling for unusual experience and a rare combination of qualities; but having got the right man there is no alternative to giving him the widest discretion in the means he uses and the direction in which he applies them — always provided he does not step outside the law".[218]

This view did not prevail for long. In 1951, the Secretary of the Cabinet, Sir Norman Brook, recommended that the responsibility for the Security Service of the nation be transferred from the Prime Minister to the Home Secretary, the gist of his proposal being contained in the following passage: "I believe that Sir Findlater Stewart exaggerated the 'defence' aspects of the Security Service. In practice the Security Service has little to do with those aspects of 'the defence of the realm' with which the Minister of Defence is concerned. And the arrangement by which the Security Service is directly responsible to the Prime Minister is now justified mainly by the fact that it enhances the status of the Service. In practice the functions of the Security Service are much more closely allied to those of the Home Office, which has the ultimate constitutional responsibility for 'defending the realm' against subversive activities and for preserving law and order. I recommend that the Security Service should in future be responsible to the Home Secretary. I believe that it would be helpful to the Director General of the Security Service to be able to turn to a senior Permanent Secretary for advice and assistance on the policy aspects of his work and on his relations with other Government Departments; and that he would receive from the permanent head of the Home Office support and guidance which the Prime Minister's secretariat is not in a position to give. The Prime Minister's personal contact with the Director General of the Security Service need not be wholly interrupted as a result of this change in Ministerial responsibility. The Prime Minister would doubtless continue to send for the Head of the Security Service from time to time, to discuss the general state of his work and particular matters which might be of specially close concern to him. And on matters of supreme importance and delicacy, the Head of the Service should always be able, at his initiation, to arrange a personal interview with the Prime Minister."[219]

The Cabinet Secretary's recommendation, we must presume, was adopted by the Cabinet for shortly afterwards the Home Secretary, Sir David Maxwell Fyfe, issued a Directive to the Director General which remains as the governing charter of the British Security Service. It deserves to be quoted in full and reads:[220]

"1. In your appointment as Director General of the Security Service you will be responsible to the Home Secretary personally. The Security Service is not, however, a part of the Home Office. On appropriate occasion you will have right of direct access to the Prime Minister.

2.   The Security Service is part of the Defence Forces of the country. Its task is the Defence of the Realm as a whole, from external and internal dangers arising from attempts at espionage and sabotage, or from actions of persons and organisations whether directed from within or without the country, which may be judged to be subversive of the State.

3.   You will take special care to see that the work of the Security Service is strictly limited to what is necessary for the purposes of this task.

4.   It is essential that the Security Service should be kept absolutely free from any political bias or influence and nothing should be done that might lend colour to any suggestion that it is concerned with interests of any particular section of the community, or with any other matter than the Defence of the Realm as a whole.

5.   No enquiry is to be carried out on behalf of any Government Department unless you are satisfied that an important public interest bearing on the Defence of the Realm, as defined in paragraph 2, is at stake.

6.   You and your staff will maintain the well-established convention whereby Ministers do not concern themselves with the detailed information which may be obtained by the Security Service in particular cases, but are furnished with such information only as may be necessary for the determination of any issue on which guidance is sought.''

We can deduce from Lord Denning's report and its acceptance by the Macmillan Government that it is now sound constitutional doctrine in Britain that, in the absence of exceptional situations, the Head of the Security Service is responsible directly to the Home Secretary and not to the Prime Minister for the efficient and proper working of the Service.[221] In normal circumstances, if anything goes wrong and questions are asked in the House of Commons it is the Home Secretary who is the Minister of the Crown held accountable to Parliament. This having been said it must be acknowledged that in the event, difficult to contemplate, that serious doubts were entertained as to the loyalty or personal activities of the Home Secretary, the Head of the Security Service might well deem it incumbent upon him to bypass the Minister and go directly to the Prime Minister. There have also been occasions in which the British Prime Minister has actively intervened in the House of Commons when matters concerning the Security Service have arisen and where, for example, the Government's desire is to stress the importance and seriousness of the events being questioned by the Opposition or where the Prime Minister chooses to treat the matter as a motion of confidence in the Government over which he presides. Both these kinds of intervention by the Prime Minister, it must be stressed, are of general application in the conduct of Government business in the Commons and are in no way a specific caveat on the Home Secretary's primary role as the Minister directly responsible to Parliament for the activities of the British Security Service.[222]

This centralization of ministerial responsibility in the one Minister, notwithstanding the continuous involvement of other Ministers in the operations of the Security Service, such as Defence, the Treasury and the Foreign Office, suggests a possible distinction of importance between Britain and Canada in terms of both constitutional theory and practice. Thus, following the establishment in 1966 of the Department of the Solicitor General of Canada with, *inter alia*, responsibility for the Royal Canadian Mounted Police including its

Security and Intelligence Directorate (later to become the Security Service), it would be understandable if the new Department and its Minister should have entertained questions as to the precise nature of the Solicitor General's control over, and responsibility for, the Security Service of Canada. Any claims that might have been advanced by the new Department for formal recognition as *the* portfolio which encompassed both supervisory powers and policy-making responsibilities for the Security Service of Canada could be said to derive support from the British constitutional theory as enunciated by the Master of the Rolls in his report on the Profumo affair.

It will have been noticed, in that report, that the formal directive setting forth the functions and duties of the Director General of the Security Service (M.I.5) was issued under the authority of the Home Secretary and not the Prime Minister. It is not known for certain whether the directive by Maxwell Fyfe was considered and approved by the Cabinet in advance of its release. In Canada, on the other hand, the general mandate to the Security Service branch of the R.C.M.P., issued on March 27, 1975, was made in the name of the Cabinet as a whole and not under the signature of the Prime Minister or the Solicitor General of Canada.[223] A similar practice, moreover, seems to have been followed whenever the Government has deemed it necessary to provide guidance to the Commissioner of the Royal Canadian Mounted Police as to the scope and manner of performing the security service functions assigned to the Force, the most recent example of Cabinet involvement in policy-making being the instruction in 1975 to cease the systematic monitoring of the Party Québecois, a legally constituted political party.[224]

In thus manifesting the active participation of the Cabinet, or a Committee of the Cabinet, in settling the broad policies to be followed by the Security Service branch of the R.C.M.P., it must follow that the Solicitor General's direct responsibilities are of a somewhat more confined nature, the precise limitations of which we shall examine more fully in a later chapter. By its very title the Cabinet Committee on Security and Intelligence reflects the essential interrelationship and overlapping that exists between the security activities and intelligence activities of government. Whether one label or the other is chosen to describe the gathering of information, the analysis of various strands of intelligence data and the preventive actions called for in the light of the total intelligence that has been collected, appears, at times, to be more a question of semantics than a well articulated set of criteria for distinguishing between the two kinds of activity. Furthermore, the distinctions sometimes drawn between domestic and foreign intelligence gathering or between defensive and offensive intelligence capabilities are not particularly helpful in the absence of agreed definitions as to what each of these activities connotes. It requires little imagination to recognize that access to the varied sources from which this kind of information is derived, and the relationships thus engendered, may involve personnel in the Departments of External Affairs, Defence, Finance or Immigration acting independently of, or working in concert with, the Security Service Branch of the R.C.M.P.

Whilst it is highly desirable that there be an ongoing collaboration between the interested branches of the Departments just mentioned, effective government requires that a central coordinating role be explicitly assigned to some defined organ in the overall machinery of government. In Canada, that part has been assigned to the Cabinet Committee on Security and Intelligence and its supporting arm, the Privy Council Office. As might be expected, the Cabinet Committee is also served by a series of subordinate inter-departmental committees, composed of public servants, which are expected to alert the ministerial members of the Cabinet if the situation warrants their attention as involving policy decisions. In his presiding role as Chairman of the Cabinet Committee on Security and Intelligence, the Prime Minister of Canada appears to have assumed a coordinating and centralizing function apropos the Security Service that has been rejected in terms of constitutional practice in Britain since 1952. The governmental machinery invoked by the Trudeau government and its immediate predecessors seems more in line with that advocated by Sir Findlater Stewart in Britain in 1945 and which was rejected several years later following the analysis of the problem by Sir Norman Brook, the Secretary to the British Cabinet. If there have been any recent changes in the security and intelligence organization of the British Government it will be important for the present Commission of Inquiry to be apprised of their nature and of the underlying reasons for any such reorganisation.

Be that as it may, particular attention must be focussed on the precept contained in the Home Secretary's directive, following his assumption of ministerial responsibility for the Security Service, to the effect that it is essential that the Service be kept absolutely free from any political bias or influence and nothing should be done that might lend substance to any suggestion that the Security Service is concerned with the interests of any particular sections of society but rather with the general public interest and the defence of the realm as a whole.[225] It will be recalled that the British Royal Commission on the Police in 1962, in examining the case for a national police force and central control by the Home Office, recognised the objections that were voiced against such a move on the ground that it would surely jeopardise the impartial exercise of a police chief's quasi-judicial functions. These included the making of decisions relating to the investigation of crime, the apprehension of offenders and the laying of criminal charges in individual cases. The criticism that centralised control by the Home Secretary would erode the essential quality of impartiality so necessary to the exercise of these particular functions was met by stressing the doctrine of ministerial accountability which would permit allegations of interference and bias to be challenged on the floor of the House of Commons.[226] The analogy was drawn with the well understood position of the Law Officers of the Crown who are required to make the same kind of decisions free of political pressures that derive from considerations of a party political nature or of narrow and sectional interests that conflict with the wider public interest of the community at large. In discharging these discretionary powers the Attorney General and Solicitor General of England have always been held accountable to Parliament.[227] We now find an echo of the same philosophy in the Home Secretary's directive to the British Security Service, in which there is implicit the recognition that any deviations from the standards set in the policy statement render the Home Secretary open to parliamentary and public accountability and the obligation to take corrective measures to ensure that there is no repetition of the same misdeeds.

At the outset of this chapter the question was posed as to how appropriate was the analogy drawn by the Pearson Government in 1966 between the responsibilities of the Home Secretary and the Solicitor General of Canada, as these relate to the police and security services functions that fall within the ambit of the respective portfolios. Reading the Canadian House of Commons debates of the time provides little evidence that the points of identity and differences, discussed in this chapter, were comprehended by any of the speakers. Still less can it be said that attention was paid to what is perhaps the most fundamental question that must be faced in defining the nature of ministerial accountability as it relates to the Solicitor General of Canada and the Home Secretary in Britain. There is no doubt that both ministers can be questioned in the respective Parliaments on matters that derive from the exercise of functions associated with the police and the security services. What has not been determined in either jurisdiction are the boundaries within which the responsible minister should exert his powers of supervision and control, and the considerations that should govern decision making in the areas of policing and the security services along the lines enunciated recently by the Minister of Justice and Attorney General of Canada with specific reference to his statutory responsibilities for prosecutions under the Official Secrets Act. We may well come to the conclusion that a sound basis exists for drawing a fairly close parallel between, on the one hand, the independence surrounding the making of what are loosely described as quasi-judicial decisions and, on the other, the Commons' duty to exert full accountability on the part of the appropriate Minister in the form of explaining and defending such decisions.

In the next chapter we shall pursue this approach a stage further by looking more closely at the boundaries that should prevail between legitimate and improper considerations in both the development of policies and the making of individual decisions within the administration of criminal law. In so doing, we shall need to consider how far issues of national security are distinguishable from questions that arise in connection with the ordinary criminal law, its enforcement and its administration. With this kind of clarification we can then hopefully proceed to consider the application in Canada of the principles of ministerial responsibility to the Ministers of the Crown in charge of the federal Department of Justice and the Department of the Solicitor General.

10. Political pressures and the independent exercise of quasi-judicial functions in policing and prosecutions — the role of police commissions

In the statement made by the Minister of Justice and Attorney General of Canada to the House of Commons on March 17, 1978,[228] explaining the reasons for his decisions whether or not prosecutions were to be launched under the Official Secrets Act,[229] Mr. Basford went to unusual lengths to expound on the parliamentary, constitutional and legal principles that guided him in the discharge of his prosecutorial discretion and made particular reference to his recent discussions with other Ministers of Justice in the Commonwealth on the office of Attorney General and its responsibilities. Addressing the Commons upon his handling of the *Cossitt* and *Toronto Sun*[230] cases, Mr. Basford declared:

> "I am aware that, since the enactment of the Official Secrets Act, this would appear to have been the first occasion in Canada where consideration has to be given to the provisions of the Official Secrets Act and the right of a member of the House to freely express his views in the House in the course of carrying on his parliamentary business. The first principle, in my view, is that there must be excluded any consideration based upon narrow, partisan views, or based upon the political consequences to me or to others. In arriving at a decision on such a sensitive issue as this, the Attorney General is entitled to seek information and advice from others but in no way is he directed by his colleagues in the government or by parliament itself. That is not say that the Attorney General is not accountable to parliament for his decisions, which he obviously is."[231]

The Minister of Justice went on to say:

> "Clearly, I am entitled to seek and obtain information from others, including my colleague, the Solicitor General, and the Commissioner of the Royal Canadian Mounted Police on the security implications of recent disclosures. This I have done. In my view, the special position of the Attorney General in this regard is clearly entrenched in our parliamentary practice. Based on these authorities and on my own experience as a member of the government for ten years, which has included my three immediate predecessors, this special position has been diligently protected in theory and in practice.[232]

The underlying philosophy enunciated in the above passages from Mr. Basford's statement is in conformity with the British constitutional theory and practice, to which I have made considerable reference in the earlier parts of this study. Despite Mr. Basford's claim, however, that his statement of policy was in keeping with the practice of his predecessors, the evidence of previous Administrations, irrespective of party affiliation, suggests the contrary. The clearest indication of the misconceptions that were being voiced in Parliament not so long ago arose out of the Government's handling in 1965 of the case involving two members of the Soviet Embassy in Ottawa who were alleged to

65

have induced a Canadian civil servant and a naturalised Canadian citizen to take part in espionage activities. The Prime Minister, Mr. Lester Pearson, was asked in the House of Commons who had the final authority to determine whether criminal proceedings were to be taken against the two Canadians; would it be the Royal Canadian Mounted Police, the Minister of Justice or one of his officials, or the Government as a whole? Mr. Pearson's reply was that "In this situation, it will be the responsibility of the Government, on the advice of the Minister of Justice",[233] a statement that he reiterated a short while later in reply to a further question by the leader of the New Democratic Party.[234] No minister, none of the leaders of the opposition parties and no member of the House of Commons saw fit to controvert this interpretation of the constitutional principles involved. And yet, as we have seen, the Prime Minister's views are a complete contradiction of the British constitutional theory of non-Cabinet interference in the determination by the Attorney General as to whether a criminal prosecution should or should not be instituted.

Again in 1965, at the time of the revelations concerning the Hal Banks extradition case and allegations of bribery on the part of the executive assistant to the Minister of Justice and the executive assistant to the Minister of Citizenship and Immigration, the Commons debates reveal that both the Government and the Opposition viewed the institution of criminal proceedings as a subject for party political debate in the most literal sense of that phrase. Thus, following the tabling of the Dorion Report, Mr. Diefenbaker is reported as asking the Minister of Justice: "As my reading of that report indicates that the bribe of $20,000, offered... for the purpose of obstructing justice, has been established, is the Government going to proceed with a prosecution in this connection?"[235] Earlier, when challenged as to why his own government, when in power, had not prosecuted the same Hal Banks for activities in connection with the blocking of the St. Lawrence Seaway by the Seafarers' Union, of which Banks was the president, Mr. Diefenbaker's reply was that his Administration had set up the Norris Commission of Inquiry, "...that Commission found the evidence and then this government prosecuted on the basis of the evidence the Norris Commission brought out."[236] One further exchange should be quoted as illustrative of the insensitivity, if not downright ignorance, on the part of both political parties to the principles at stake. Immediately after the Leader of the Opposition had sought to make political capital out of the Pearson Government's inactivity regarding the controversial Hal Banks, the Minister of Labour (Mr. MacEachen) inquired why the Diefenbaker Government had refused to prosecute Banks on facts that were widely publicised in August 1957. Mr. Diefenbaker's response is illuminating. "My recollection" he said "is that we did everything we could to be sure that if we prosecuted we would have a case".[237] Although not stated in so many words, the supposition that the decision was one that would have been taken by the Cabinet, and not left to the independent judgement of the Attorney General of Canada, is hard to resist.

The same theme is to be discerned in the remarks of Mr. Guy Favreau when, speaking as Minister of Justice and Attorney General of Canada on the same subject of bringing Hal Banks before the criminal courts, the Minister stated: "...in 1963, as soon as the Norris report was published, as soon as the government could do something, legal action was taken and complaints were lodged after the government had retained the best Toronto and Montreal lawyers. So, this government is the first to do something about Mr. Banks; this government is the first to assume its responsibilities and prosecute Mr. Banks with the results we know ... I must inform the House that, if necessary, this government will continue to act in the same way concerning Banks or anyone else who must be prosecuted".[238]

This approach is a far cry from the classic exposition of the correct constitutional principles relating to the functions of the Attorney General, made in the English House of Commons by Sir Hartley Shawcross in 1954 and again by Prime Minister Macmillan in 1959. Mr. Favreau's apparent acceptance of the position that decisions to prosecute, even in cases of industrial sabotage, were the responsibility of the government and not that of the Attorney General is to be condemned as a distortion of the proper principles and an abdication of the special role accorded to the office of Attorney General in administering the criminal law. Any claims by a Prime Minister or Premier of a province of the right of government to determine whether or not charges are to be brought in the criminal courts is nothing less than an abuse of power.

All the more reason, therefore, to be concerned about remarks attributed to the present Prime Minister, Mr. Joe Clark, during the recent general election campaign. Speaking in the course of a television interview, and not from a prepared script, the then Leader of the Opposition said that, if he became Prime Minister, he would prosecute any Liberal Cabinet Minister found responsible for alleged illegalities by the R.C.M.P.; "If legal action was called for I would certainly not grant an exception to anyone for the consequences of breaking the law."[239] Allowance must be made for the fact that this statement was made in the context of a political campaign. Nevertheless, it will be seen as in keeping with similar views expressed by earlier leaders of the major political parties in the House of Commons and which have yet to be disavowed.

Earlier in this study reference was made to the partial resolution by the Supreme Court of Canada of the controversy surrounding the constitutionality of the 1968-69 amendment to the definition of "Attorney General" contained in section 2 of the Criminal Code. The *Hauser* case adverted to the issue of concurrent or exclusive jurisdiction of the Attorney General of Canada to institute certain classes of criminal proceedings but the Supreme Court Justices made no reference to another aspect of the section 2 amendment that is germane to the present discussion of the independence of the Attorney General of Canada in matters of criminal prosecution. I refer to the language of the Criminal Code that reads:

" 'Attorney General' means the Attorney General or Solicitor General of a province in which proceedings to which this Act applies are taken and, with respect to...

(b) *proceedings instituted at the instance of the Government of Canada and conducted by or on behalf of that Government* in respect of a violation of or conspiracy to violate any Act of the Parliament of Canada or a regulation made thereunder other than this act,
means the Attorney General of Canada...."

It will be noted that the italicised words embody the constitutional understanding that is reflected in the passages quoted above from the speeches in the House of Commons of Prime Ministers Pearson and Diefenbaker and at least one previous occupant of the offices of Minister of Justice and Attorney General of Canada. My criticism of these earlier expositions of the proper constitutional principle in matters of criminal prosecutions extends no less to the legislative language introduced into the Criminal Code when amending the definition of "Attorney General".

It might be argued that what is envisaged in the italicised words "instituted at the instance of the Government of Canada" is simply that the original information should be sworn by an agent of the Government of Canada, as opposed to a municipal or provincial peace officer.[240] Such a restrictive interpretation ignores the ensuing words wherein what is contemplated is that the criminal prosecution is "conducted by or on behalf of that Government". It is my contention that the Attorney General's authority in this regard derives from the Crown and is inherently an exercise of the prerogative powers of the Crown. Any attempt to invest the Crown's prosecutorial powers in the Government of Canada (or for that matter in the Government of a province) is to open the gates to the kind of partisan political abuses about which I have spoken and against which the independent nature of the office of the Attorney General is the constitutional shield.

All the more reason, therefore, for welcoming the firm stand taken by the Minister of Justice, Mr. Ron Basford, in the Official Secrets Act cases last year, in which he stated unequivocally that "In arriving at a decision on such a sensitive issue as this, the Attorney General is entitled to seek information and advice from others but in no way is he directed by his colleagues in the government or by parliament itself".[241] In this passage is contained the nub of the problem. An Attorney General who seeks to sustain his privileged constitutional status as the guardian of the public interest in the widest sense of that term may seek, and frequently would be seriously at fault in failing to do so, advice from whatever quarter, ministerial or otherwise, that may help to illuminate the decision confronting him. What is absolutely forbidden is the subjection by the Attorney General of his discretionary authority to the edict of the Prime Minister or the Cabinet or Parliament itself. Parliament has the right to question and criticise the Law Officers. It does not have the right to direct them in the discharge of their constitutional duties.[242]

Applying these considerations to the cases before him in the *Cossitt* affair, the Attorney General of Canada further emphasised that, in exercising his discretion as to whether or not he should consent to a prosecution under the Official Secrets Act, it was incumbent upon him to ensure that the widest possible public interests of Canada were taken into account. In this task he had to balance the rights, privileges, traditions and immunities so necessary for the proper functioning of parliament, and the doubts that exist as to the application of parliamentary privilege to statements made by M.P.'s outside the House of Commons.[243] It was Mr. Basford's view that he should not grant his consent to a prosecution unless the case was free from substantial doubt. Accordingly, he announced his decision not to proceed against the individual Member of Parliament whose disclosures had prompted the Attorney General into action. Conversely, the first Law Officer of the Crown said that, in the case of the Toronto Sun, he had due regard to the principle of freedom of the press which did not embody absolute rights. Rather it must be exercised pursuant to the rule of law. Parliament not having seen fit to extend to any other person or body the rights, privileges or immunities that are accorded by law to parliament and its members, the Attorney General concluded that, after balancing the various competing interests, he should issue his fiat for the launching of criminal proceedings against the Toronto newspaper, and its editor and publisher.[244]

This may be an appropriate point to raise a point of parliamentary practice that calls for rectification. At the end of his statement to the House in the Official Secrets Act cases, the Minister of Justice made reference to the fact that in arriving at his decisions he had sought the opinion of the officers of the Department of Justice and that they had concurred in the result.[245] On previous occasions, and by many of Mr. Basford's predecessors in similar circumstances, the views of the departmental officials in the Department of Justice have been referred to as the opinions of "the Law Officers of the Crown".[246] So much so that the habit has developed to the point that it is the lawyers on the permanent establishment of the Department of Justice, and not the Attorney General and Solicitor General, who have come to be regarded in Canada as occupying the special position historically associated with the Law Officers of the Crown. Such misuse of the term can be misleading and tends to obscure the source of the responsibilities exercisable in the constitution by the Attorney General, both federally and provincially, and, at least until the 1966 reorganisation of the federal government, by the Solicitor General of Canada. The occupants of these offices and they alone are entitled to be addressed as the Law Officers of the Crown. Any parliamentary usage to the contrary should be discontinued, otherwise difficulties may arise one day in defining the scope of the Law Officers' ministerial responsibilities.

Another misunderstanding that needs to be clarified concerns the use of the pejorative word 'politics' in the context of police and prosecutorial decision-making. This question has arisen in its sharpest and most controversial form when the Attorney General or his agents are faced with making prosecutorial decisions. These include not only judgments as to whether or not to initiate a prosecution but, an even more sensitive issue, whether to withdraw or discontinue criminal proceedings which are in progress. I endeavoured to address this problem in my discussion paper for the Commonwealth Attorneys General at their meeting in Winnipeg in late 1977.[247] What seems to be uppermost in the minds of those who place a high premium on safeguarding the independent exercise of prosecutorial decision making is the vital necessity of resisting improper political pressures. If, however, misunderstandings are to be avoided and workable boundaries drawn between those political considerations to which it is proper for an Attorney General or Director of Public Prosecutions to have regard and those which should not be entertained it is essential that we clarify the precise meaning accorded to the term "politics" when applied to different stages in the criminal process.

What is evident, in nearly all the discussions of this central issue, is the fact that the term is invoked as if it possessed only one connotation which is objectionable *per se*. It is my contention that there exists a fundamental demarcation that needs to be constantly borne in mind when analyzing the application of the doctrine of ministerial accountability in the area of policing and prosecutions. We begin with the proposition, to which Mr. Basford subscribed unequivocally in his Official Secrets Act statement, that anything savouring of personal advancement or sympathy felt by an Attorney General, or Solicitor General towards a political colleague or supporter (or opponent) or which relates to the political fortune of his party and the government in power should not be countenanced if adherence to the principles of impartiality and integrity are to be publicly manifested. This does not mean that the Attorney General in the realm of prosecutions, or the Solicitor General in the area of policing, should not have regard to political considerations in the non-partisan interpretation of the term "politics". Thus, it might be thought that there are legitimate political grounds for taking into account such matters as the maintenance of harmonious international relations between states, the reduction of strife between ethnic groups, the maintenance of industrial peace and generally the interests of the public at large in deciding whether (or when) to initiate criminal proceedings or whether (and when) to terminate a prosecution that is in progress.

All these broad political considerations, whether domestic or international in character, must be seen to involve the wider public interest that benefits the population at large rather than any single political group or factional interest. In my perception of the term, "partisan politics" has a much narrower focus and is designed to protect or advance the retention of constitutional power by the incumbent government and its political supporters. It is the intervention of political considerations in this latter sense that should have no place in the making of prosecutorial decisions by the Attorney General of Canada or in the making of policing or security decisions by the Solicitor General of Canada. Adherence to the same doctrine should be universally evident on the part of the Commissioner of the Royal Canadian Mounted Police and the officers of the force when executing any general mandates issued by the Government.

The events and parliamentary debates which were referred to at the beginning of this chapter point to a different interpretation of what is proper in terms of the political considerations that should govern the exercise of the Attorney General's discretionary power with respect to possible prosecutions. Since evidence is not readily forthcoming as to the principles and practice that guided earlier Attorneys General of Canada, it is difficult to assert that the Basford exposition in relation to the *Cossitt* and *Toronto Sun* cases represents a dramatic departure from the previous constitutional theory in Canada on the nature of the Law Officers' accountability to Parliament. If anything, it might be claimed that no clear exposition of any theory existed until very recently and that attention to the pertinent British constitutional precedents has only latterly occupied the parliamentary forums.

If any conclusion is to be derived from the ministerial statements quoted earlier from the *Hal Banks* affair in 1965, it is the uncritical assumption that some prosecutorial decisions will naturally assume a high political profile because of the position which the accused enjoys in society, the circumstances that give rise to possible criminal charges or the political consequences that will flow from the outcome of the trial. There is good reason to suppose that prior to the Basford statement in 1978 most Ministers of the Crown would have viewed their involvement in the disposition of such prosecutorial questions in Cabinet as a natural application of the principle of collective responsibility for unpalatable political decisions. In making these decisions it should not be assumed that the Cabinet would necessarily be governed by politically partisan motives. At the same time, it would be unrealistic not to envisage situations in which, in the absence of any clearly understood constitutional prohibition against the referral by the Attorney General of prosecutorial matters for decision by the Cabinet or any group of Ministers or the Prime Minister, partisan influences would rise to the surface and prevail in whatever decision ultimately emerged.

What is applicable to Cabinet decision-making is equally associated with the deliberations of Parliament and the Legislative Assemblies of the Provinces. Perhaps because of the strongly embedded Canadian tradition of regarding the parliamentary system as essentially an exercise in partisan politics, it may be thought to be impractical to attempt to imbue these assemblies with a concept of impartiality that is so foreign to their interpretation of their customary functions. The issue, however, should not be looked upon in terms of customary practice alone or even in seeking accord with the practicalities of existing governmental and parliamentary practice. The issue must be lifted on to a higher plane and the question posed — in what form is the broadest public interest likely to be served when the quality of our system of criminal justice is at stake? Are all questions that savour of political ramifications to be treated alike and made subject to the will of the Government in power and to the collective responsibility of the Cabinet? Or are there certain areas of ministerial responsibility, especially that of the Attorney General's prerogative discretion with respect to criminal prosecutions, which require that the Prime Minister and other Ministers in the Government refrain from becoming directly involved in the final decision that is made? Later on I shall argue that this doctrine should properly be extended to those situations in which a Minister (including the Attorney General) is charged by express statutory provision with the exercise of a discretionary power. If any true meaning is to be given to the discharge of this kind of statutory discretion the collegial system of Cabinet involvement must be confined to a consultative role. Such consultation, however, must never be allowed to become dictation.

I venture to state that nothing is more calculated to engender public disillusionment with the criminal justice system and its constituent parts, — especially the police, the security service and the Crown prosecutors — than disclosures indicating a susceptibility to extraneous pressures. The greatest safeguard against the sullying of these pillars of justice will be found in the integrity and sense of fundamental values that are nurtured by the individuals who have to administer the several parts of the system. Without these personal qualities any constitutional machinery or doctrine is extremely vulnerable. The responsibility of Parliament, Government and of individual Ministers, is to create the kind of administrative machinery that will assist, rather than obstruct, the fulfillment of those ideals which are essential to maintaining public confidence in the criminal justice system.

I intend to return to this particular theme at the conclusion of this study when a closer look will be taken at the extent of ministerial supervision which is necessary to ensure the proper degree of accountability in the public sphere. Central to this problem in the police and security service areas is the harmonizing of an adequate flow of information with regard to the policies and procedures of the agencies for which a Minister is constitutionally responsible, coupled with a determination on the part of the Minister and his senior departmental officials to eschew any interference with the making of those kinds of quasi-judicial decisions about which I have spoken earlier.

At this point it may be useful to note the emergence, in most of the Canadian provinces, of police commissions, which are intended *at the provincial level* to act as a buffer between the executive branch of government, including the Minister and his departmental officials, and the chiefs of police in running their respective forces on a day to day basis, and, *at the municipal level*, to keep a healthy distance between the police chief and the elected local politicians who are appointed to serve as representatives of the municipal government on the local police commission or police committee. From time to time, questions are properly raised as to the ability of those members of police boards whose appointment rests in the hands of the provincial Cabinet, and who generally constitute a majority of the board members, to adequately fulfill the independence associated with the method and source of their appointment. Empirical evidence derived from the experience of these relationships is not normally available, the general public having to content themselves with revelations or impressions that derive from the news media's handling of controversial events. Considerably more evidence needs to be brought to light of subservience to the will of the provincial Executive before action is taken to replace the existing "buffer" principle with an alternative model in which the elected local politicians would once again reign supreme in the running of a police department.

The experience to date of these provincial initiatives may not be wholly irrelevant to the special problems experienced in the federal Department of the Solicitor General and its mandate with respect to the Royal Canadian Mounted Police. Commencing with the Ontario Police Commission which was set up under that province's Police Act of 1962,[248] Quebec followed suit in 1968,[249] then came Alberta in 1971,[250] Manitoba in 1971,[251] Nova Scotia in

1974,[252] Saskatchewan in 1974,[253] British Columbia in 1974[254] and New Brunswick in 1977.[255] It is not proposed to conduct in this study a comparative analysis of the statutory powers and duties of the respective commissions. It must suffice to quote the provisions in the Ontario legislation, which enumerates the functions of the first such provincial Police Commission. According to section 41 of the Ontario Police Act, 1962,

"(1) It is the function of the Commission,

  (a) to maintain a system of statistical records and research studies of criminal occurrences and matters related thereto for the purpose of aiding the police forces in Ontario;

  (b) to consult with and advise boards of commissioners of police, police committees of municipal councils and other police authorities and chiefs of police on all matters relating to police and policing;

  (c) to provide to boards of commissioners of police, police committees of municipal councils and other police authorities and chiefs of police information and advice respecting the management and operation of police forces, techniques in handling special problems and other information calculated to assist;

  (d) through its members and advisers, to conduct a system of visits to the police forces in Ontario;

  (e) to require municipalities to provide such lock-ups as the Commission may determine;

  (f) to assist in co-ordinating the work and efforts of the police forces in Ontario;

  (g) to determine whether a police force is adequate and whether a municipality is discharging its responsibility for the maintenance of law and order;

  (h) to inquire into any matter regarding the designation of a village or township under subsection 4 of section 2 and, after a hearing, to make recommendations therefor to the Minister;

  (i) to operate the Ontario Police College;

  (j) subject to the approval of the Minister, to establish and require the installation of an inter-communication system for the police forces in Ontario and to govern its operation and procedures;

  (k) to conduct investigations in accordance with the provisions of this Act;

  (l) to hear and dispose of appeals by members of police forces in accordance with this Act and the regulations; and

  (m) to exercise the powers and perform the duties conferred and imposed upon it by this Act.

(2) Subject to the approval of the Minister, the Commission may, by order, regulate or prohibit the use of any equipment by a police force in Ontario or its members."

In the debate that ensued following the introduction of this measure, the Premier of Ontario, Mr. John Robarts, declared that "The Commission is designed to be completely independent of any control by any department of government".[256] Given the dependence, however, of the Ontario Police Commission, and its provincial counterparts, on Government for the funds it needs to conduct its operations, it is impossible to ignore a touch of rhetoric in the Premier's remarks. The emphasis in the above list of Commission functions, I suggest, is closely akin to the Home Office's expanded responsibilities, since 1964, for the efficiency of the various police forces in Britain where, it will be recalled, the Royal Commission on the Police, in its 1962 report, drew a sharp distinction between, (1) the quasi-judicial functions of a police force — in matters of investigation, arrest and the laying of charges — and (2) the allocation of police resources and measures adopted by a police chief in the management and deployment of the force under his command. It is conceived that the same distinction is inherent in the ambit of responsibilities delegated to the Ontario and other Police Commissions, notwithstanding certain differences in the language of the respective provincial statutes.

The same philosophy, it is maintained, should govern the interpretation of the provision in the Ontario Police Act which deals with the power and duties of the Ontario Provincial Police and which states in section 42: "There shall be a Commissioner of the Ontario Provincial Police Force who shall be appointed by the Lieutenant Governor in Council; Subject to the direction of the Ontario Police Commission as approved by the Minister, the Commissioner has the general control and administration of the Ontario Provincial Police Force and the employees connected therewith". Apart from Quebec which also has its own provincial police force, the other provinces, generally speaking, have contracted with the federal government for the Royal Canadian Mounted Police to carry out the duties normally undertaken by municipal police forces. The question naturally arises how far is a provincial police commission empowered to exercise the degree of supervision or control, connoted in the Ontario Police Act with respect to the Ontario Provincial Police, in relation to the R.C.M.P. force that operates under contract to the provincial government.[257] In their Police Acts Alberta and Manitoba have solved the dilemma by resort to a compromise that may yet prove to be unworkable. According to the law of these provinces, any inquiry into the activities of a member of the R.C.M.P., operating within their jurisdictional boundaries, is to be undertaken by the Attorney General of the province and the report of its findings must be submitted to the Commissioner of the Force. Any disciplinary measures that may be called for are to be decided jointly by the Commissioner and the Attorney General of the province.[258] Given an atmosphere of mutual trust and confidence such a system can work efficiently and unobtrusively. The real problems surface when there is a division of opinion derived from a difference in philosophy or in the development of a mood of suspicion that results from the handling of individual cases.

At the level of municipal policing the Ontario Police Act confers upon the provincial police commission what, in normal circumstances, are essentially advisory and consultative functions. These are illustrated by the provisions which require the Commission, first, "to consult with and advise boards of commissioners of police, police committees of municipal councils and other police authorities and chiefs of police on all matters related to police and policing"[259] and, secondly, to provide to the same bodies and individual police chiefs "information and advice respecting the management and operation of police forces, techniques in handling special problems and other information calculated to assist."[260]

Alongside these advisory functions, however, is the not inconsiderable power to have the Ontario Provincial Police take over the policing of a municipality in the event that the municipality has failed to maintain an adequate police force.[261] Also the Ontario Police Commission is empowered, on its own initiative, to investigate or to set up a formal inquiry under the Public Inquiries Act into "the conduct of or the performance of duties by any chief of police, other police officer ... the administration of any police force, the system of policing any municipality, and the police needs of any municipality ..."[262] Both of these statutory powers confer effective controls that go well beyond an advisory and consultative role for the Commission.

In estimating the dangers of interference and pressures being exerted against the members of a police force, from the police chief down to the ordinary constable, what must be identified is the composition and powers of the local police authority. At least in Ontario, the principle has been adhered to in the larger municipalities that the members of the police commission or board should consist of a mixture of elected representatives, drawn from the municipal council, and members appointed by the Lieutenant-Governor in Council, prominent among whom are usually members of the lower judiciary. The majority of the members are to be drawn from outside the ranks of the elected representatives, a situation that has been assailed vigorously in the editorial columns of some of Canada's leading newspapers. The existing framework in Ontario, in my view, provides the right kind of checks and balances that are so necessary to ensure the impartial application of the criminal law. If some changes are felt to be necessary in the composition of these local supervisory bodies, such as the range of persons who are appointed and with less concentration on a judicial background,[263] great care must be exercised not to mutilate the essential buffer principle which is presently reflected in the notion of a police commission or board that stands between the Minister and the individual police chief, however large or small the police force under his command.

The other central provision in the Ontario Police Act is that contained in section 17 which declares: "...the Board is responsible for the policing and maintenance of law and order in the municipality and the members of the police force are subject to the government by the board and shall obey its lawful directions". It is not possible to express an informed judgment as to how far individual police boards or commissions are prepared to invoke the literal application of this potentially insidious provision. There is nothing in the section to counsel restraint or to point to the damage to public confidence that is capable of being effected by interference with the more sensitive decisions that must be made daily by the police chief and his colleagues out in the field. It is, therefore, of paramount importance that the right attitudes be instilled in those who exercise the statutory powers of direction. The example set at the top in the person of the Solicitor General of Ontario and his counterparts in other provinces can be crucial. By the same token the Solicitor General of Canada must be seen to be conscious of the limitations surrounding the exercise of his mandate as the minister responsible to the Prime Minister and his colleagues, and above all to Parliament, for the judicious application of his powers and duties with respect to the Royal Canadian Mounted Police. How best can our constitutional and parliamentary system ensure the maintenance of these standards of impartiality and accountability becomes the next question to be studied in this paper.

11. The dimensions of ministerial responsibility — constitutional theory and practice

The modern realities of administering a Government and being the Minister in charge of a major Department, have led to some serious questioning as to the current constitutional meaning of ministerial responsibility. It is not necessary to look further than the series of debates and question periods in the Canadian House of Commons in recent times to perceive the degree of confusion as to the nature and limits of this doctrine that exists among parliamentarians. Inevitably, the gulf in its interpretation between the Government and the Opposition parties has been transmitted into the public domain. Simplistic attitudes become hardened in the process and doubts are cultivated as to the effectiveness of the entire parliamentary system. Especially is this so when the yardstick of effectiveness is viewed exclusively in terms of extracting ministerial resignations following upon allegations and proof of ministerial ineptitude.

It is vital that proper boundaries of the relevant constitutional principles be recognised and receive universal acceptance by all political parties. One of the healthiest aspects of the current investigation into certain R.C.M.P. activities is the concentration of attention that is being accorded to what is sensed to be a special application of the doctrine to the Solicitor General of Canada as the minister responsible for all the functions connected with the R.C.M.P. including its security service responsibilities. In previous sections of this study I have drawn attention to the unique ministerial role that the Attorney General, federally and provincially, is expected to perform in the field of criminal law and it will be necessary in this chapter to again pay special attention to the particular application of questions of ministerial responsibility to the Minister of Justice of Canada when acting in his capacity as the Attorney General of Canada.

We must first begin by recognising that there does not exist a single doctrine of ministerial responsibility. Whether we are talking in terms of British or Canadian constitutional law the phrase is properly used in a number of different senses. Since, historically speaking, the individual responsibility of Ministers of the Crown preceded the introduction of collective responsibility, with its emphasis on party discipline and the government's devotion to the cause of self preservation, I intend to concentrate initially on the former meaning. It is far from clear to me that the substitution of terms like "accountability" and "answerability" in place of "responsibility" casts any greater light *per se* on the precise meaning that is involved. There is, however, some advantage to be gained in keeping distinct a minister's responsibility for the policies of his Department and the extent that a minister is held accountable for individual acts and decisions that are taken within the Department by officials of whatever seniority. There is also nowadays a less important distinction that divides a minister's legal and political responsibilities in the exercise of his ministerial functions. It will be recalled that Professor A.V. Dicey included within his interpretation of the rule of law the principle that ministers and public officials alike were personally liable in law before the ordinary courts for any civil wrong perpetrated upon the private rights of a citizen, unless it could be shown that such infringement was authorised by express statutory powers.[264] This strict legal doctrine has long since been supplanted by legislation, in both Canada and Britain, which permits an aggrieved citizen to sue the Crown directly for wrongs committed in the exercise of a Minister's statutory or conventional powers or which derive from acts done in the name of the Department.[265]

Political responsibility is the essence of the concept of ministerial responsibility. In the individual sense of that term it means that a Minister's tenure of his office is dependent on the judgment of various "tribunals" as to his handling of the multifarious matters that derive from his portfolio. It is important at this stage to recognise the relative significance of these bodies before whom a minister can be brought to account, metaphorically if not literally in the political sense of that term. Most frequently, attention is directed to the House of Commons in which the minister can be subjected to critical exposure by the Opposition during the question period of each daily session. Alternatively, he may have to meet the challenge contained in a formal motion of censure. The cry for the resignation of a minister often spearheads the efforts of the Opposition parties but, as we shall see shortly, there do not exist any clear cut conventions in either British or Canadian constitutional law as to the circumstances in which there is an imperative duty on the part of a Minister to tender his resignation when he is in political trouble.

In an attempt to explain the present day understanding on the subject of ministerial resignations Professor S.A. de Smith, writing in 1971, perspicaciously focussed attention on the personal and political relationship that exists between a Minister who is at the centre of a political storm and the Prime Minister who appointed him in the first place. "Unless the Prime Minister" de Smith wrote[266] "is willing to stand by the Minister under attack — and in this context the personal authority of a Prime Minister is of great importance — a Minister may choose, and has not infrequently chosen in recent years, to brazen out appalling indiscretions, gross errors and omissions, plans gone awry and revelations of disastrous mismanagement within his Department. If the Opposition is allowed time to make a vote of censure, or if a supply day is selected for the purpose of moving a motion to reduce the Minister's salary, the Minister can confidently expect to emerge triumphant in the division lobbies, with members voting strictly along party lines. Yet his victory may prove to be pyrrhic and ephemeral. The Prime Minister may shift him to another office carrying less prestige in the next ministerial reshuffle; he may kick him upstairs to the Lords; he may quietly call for the Minister's resignation at a moment less embarrassing for the Government, or gratefully accept a half-hearted offer of resignation if it comes. A Minister who is incapable of explaining and justifying his conduct of affairs persuasively in the face of a hostile Opposition, or to the satisfaction of independent political commentators, is a liability to the Government and the party."

Given the fact that "Every Cabinet Minister is in a sense the Prime Minister's agent — his assistant"[267] it follows that the ultimate sanction of demanding the resignation of a recalcitrant minister who has become a political liability rests squarely in the hands of the Prime Minister. This is clearly the constitutional theory but it would be wrong to give this statement too literal and automatic an application. There appears to be a universal acceptance of the proposition that where personal culpability on the part of a Minister is shown, in the form of private or public conduct that is generally regarded as unbecoming and unworthy of a Minister of the Crown, the expectation is that the Minister should tender his resignation to the Prime Minister.[268] It is only necessary to cite the recent example of Mr. Francis Fox, the former Solicitor General of Canada, to illustrate the dimensions of this aspect of the wider doctrine.[269] In England, it will be recalled that Mr. John Profumo resigned his portfolio in 1963 as Secretary of State for War after it became known that he had lied to the House of Commons in rebuttal of allegations concerning his private life.[270] Other precedents that come to mind, and which are usually invoked to define the expansiveness of the convention, involved Mr. J.H. Thomas in 1936,[271] and Dr. Hugh Dalton in 1947,[272] who resigned as Chancellor of the Exchequer after it was revealed that they had prematurely disclosed parts of their Budget proposals. Significantly, in the case of Dr. Dalton there was no suggestion of improper motives but rather an exuberant indiscretion. No distinction, however, was made between the two cases. In Canada, as already adverted to in this study, Mr. Guy Favreau tendered his resignation in 1965 following the Dorion Commission of Inquiry and the Commissioner's criticisms of his handling of the police investigation and consequential prosecutions.[273]

In every one of these precedents it will be observed that the culpability of the Minister was personal in every sense of the word, thus leaving the strong suggestion that the closer the allegations of misconduct or incompetence are laid to the door of the Minister's private office or personal life the greater will be the pressures to submit his resignation as the political price demanded by the constitution. To say this is not conclusive of the outcome of such a move. It still remains open to the Prime Minister to refuse to accept the resignation or to delay its acceptance until it can be accomplished with a minimum of political damage to the Government and the party in power. We do not need to look further than the precedents associated with what became known as "the Judges' affair" in Quebec in 1975, as a result of which the Prime Minister accepted the resignation of Mr. Ouellet, the Minister of Consumer and Corporate Affairs,[274] but declined to take the same step with reference to the respected and senior member of the Cabinet, Mr. Bud Drury, then President of the Treasury Board.[275] Uppermost in the mind of any Prime Minister when estimating the venality of ministerial indiscretions are the political consequences that will flow from the alternative courses of action open to him. These consequences will be measured both in their short term and long term impact. Furthermore, whatever position the Prime Minister finally adopts he must be confident that he carries the support of his parliamentary caucus and his political party. This interaction between colleagues, within and without the Cabinet, is constant and no Prime Minister can afford to exercise his autocratic powers with complete insensitivity to the personal feelings of the resigning minister, the minister who is dismissed or those who remain to serve as Cabinet and political colleagues.

Cabinet solidarity, after all, is one of the principal foundations of retaining governmental power. This is sometimes expressed differently and in more rhetorical language to the effect that the collective responsibility of the Cabinet to the House of Commons is a democratic bulwark of the British Constitution.[276] By the same token, the doctrine of collective responsibility is said to be of equal importance in Canadian constitutional law.[277] Theoretically, this means that a Government must maintain a majority in the House of Commons if it is to remain in power. In modern constitutional practice, however adverse the Commons' voting might be on non-budgetary matters or at different stages in the passage of a Bill these votes do not, in themselves, call for the resignation of an Administration or the dissolution of Parliament. It would have to be a defeat on a fiscal matter of supply such as the budget resolutions or a specific motion of non-confidence to force a Prime Minister to admit defeat at the hands of the House of Commons and thus require him to advise the Governor General to dissolve Parliament and call a general election.

To safeguard the Government's majority in the Commons, the Prime Minister and his Cabinet must place a premium on a constant show of public unanimity. Any Minister who wishes to carry into the public arena his dissenting views, notwithstanding his having properly advanced the same opinions within Cabinet to nil effect, cannot expect to keep his place within the Government and must resign. If political practice is sometimes seen as deviating from the above constitutional theory, and there are several instances that spring to mind within my own memory, it can best be understood on the grounds of political expediency in which the degree of opposition to Cabinet policies ventilated publicly by an individual Minister has to be judged by the Prime Minister in varying shades and emphases. As Professor de Smith puts it:[278] "It is open to the Prime Minister to condone a verbal indiscretion by a colleague, and even to overlook a studied refusal by a colleague to offer positive commendation of a policy which he dislikes, though the line between half-hearted formal acquiescence and hints of real disagreement may wear thin. But in this century only for a few months in 1932 has the convention been expressly waived, on the issue of tariff protection and under a coalition Government; this experiment was not a success, and despite occasional deviations from the norm since that time, the general principle is clear."

The corollary to this aspect of collective ministerial responsibility has been described by the same author in this fashion: "Just as Ministers are expected to be loyal to their colleagues, so they can reasonably claim to be entitled to the loyalty of their colleagues if they run into public criticism in implementing agreed Cabinet policies. If they implement them badly, or if they incur criticism as a result of purely departmental failings or indications of personal ineptitude, they will not have any corresponding claim to corporate solidarity".[279] Earlier in this chapter I suggested that there was some advantage to be gained in this discussion if a minister's individual responsibility for the *policies* of his Department were to be kept distinct from the degree of accountability that could be exerted by the House of Commons with respect to individual *acts* and *decisions* taken within the Department by the public officials in pursuit of such policies. When reference is made to the policies that guide the day to day administration of a Department it goes without saying that the major configurations of these policies will normally have been submitted to the Cabinet for approval or cleared in advance between the Minister concerned and the Prime Minister. Occasionally, this reference will be a preliminary to the introduction of a programme requiring legislative action in which the full machinery of Cabinet committees may have to be traversed. On other occasions, the policy issues that arise may derive from the choice of alternative courses of action any one of which may be sanctioned by existing legislation. Reference to the Cabinet for its stamp of approval is the surest way in which a Minister can lean on the collective responsibility of his ministerial colleagues led by the Prime Minister.

Apart altogether from the more controversial questions that may instigate a Minister to involve the Cabinet, with its ever pressing agenda of urgent items submitted by other Departments, there are internal issues which a Minister and his senior officials must deal with as policy questions knowing that the results of their decisions may erupt unexpectedly into the political arena. Of all the pressing problems that arise in the present context none is more indeterminate than the extent to which a Minister should be held accountable for the questionable acts and decisions of the officials in his Department. There is no denying the growth and complexity of modern day governmental activities in which most Departments are microcosms of the whole enormous edifice. No matter how industrious or intellectually able the individual Minister may be, the days are long past when he can be expected to exercise that degree of close supervision over the working of his Department that justified holding the Minister personally responsible for anything that went amiss within the Departmental sphere of operations.

In Britain, the need to develop working guidelines for invoking this aspect of individual ministerial responsibility has resulted in several authoritative statements that we should look at with a view to determining their transferability to the Canadian constitutional scene. Speaking in 1956, on the occasion of a debate concerning the British Secret Service, Mr. Hugh Gaitskell emphasised the basic assumption that "the operations of these services are ultimately and effectively controlled by Ministers or a Minister".[280] Speaking with particular reference to the application of ministerial responsibility to the activities of the Secret Service Mr. Gaitskell continued: "It is the custom for Ministers to cover up any decision by a civil servant; that is to say, normally the Minister not merely takes responsibility but appears to have taken that decision himself, whether, in fact, he did so or not. Even when this is not done and, of course, there are quite a number of occasions when it would be pedantic to insist that it should be done, when, in fact, a Minister comes to the House, and says, 'One of my officials made a mistake', thereby implying that he, the Minister, was not directly responsible for that mistake, nevertheless it is a sound and vital constitutional principle that the Minister takes responsibility for what has happened. That is a principle which I venture to say is fundamental to our democracy, because if we were to depart from it, it would imply that the Civil Service in some way or other was independent and not answerable to this House. Of course, the extent to which we condemn a Minister for an act of one of his officers, or a failure by one of his officers, obviously depends on the circumstances. There are minor occasions when a Minister admits that something has gone wrong and the House accepts it and the matter is left... [N]one of us would ask that the Prime Minister should disclose what ought not to be disclosed... Subject to this... it is the duty of any Opposition... to prove any weakness or what appears to be blunders or mistakes in Government administration.''[281]

The *Crichel Down case* in Britain in 1954 is frequently cited as supportive of the principle that a minister's resignation is called for where allegations of maladministration on the part of senior officials in his department are confirmed. Sir Thomas Dugdale, the Minister concerned, rejected suggestions that officials in the Ministry of Agriculture had wilfully misled him but readily admitted there were inaccuracies and deficiencies in the information given to him on the basis of which he reached his decision regarding the disposition of certain land over which his Ministry had control. The conduct of the civil servants concerned was the subject of a public inquiry and a report which administered a public reprimand to some of the officials concerned. After rendering his report to Parliament on the affair the Minister of Agriculture announced his resignation.[282]

Whether this step was called for in the circumstances of that case is debatable. At least one authoritative writer has claimed that it was not demanded by constitutional convention and pointed out that "other Ministers have not sought to emulate him by exacting the supreme political penalty on themselves".[283] In the debate that ensued following the announcement of Dugdale's resignation an important statement of constitutional principles was made by the Home Secretary, Sir David Maxwell Fyfe, the same incumbent, incidentally, who set forth the directive to the British Security Service that continues to govern its operations. The statement deserves to be quoted *in extenso*. It reads as follows:[284]

> "...There has been criticism that the principle (of Ministerial responsibility) operates so as to oblige Ministers to extend total protection to their officials and to endorse their acts, and to cause the position that civil servants cannot be called to account and are effectively responsible to no one. That is a position which I believe is quite wrong... It is quite untrue that well-justified public criticism of the actions of civil servants cannot be made on a suitable occasion. The position of the civil servant is that he is wholly and directly responsible to his Minister. It is worth stating again that he holds his office 'at pleasure' and can be dismissed at any time by the Minister; and that power is none the less real because it is seldom used. The only exception relates to a small number of senior posts, like permanent secretary, deputy secretary, and principal officer, where, since 1920, it has been necessary for the Minister to consult the Prime Minister, as he does on appointment.

I would like to put the different categories where different considerations apply... (I)n the case where there is an explicit order by a Minister, the Minister must protect the civil servant who has carried out his order. Equally, where the civil servant acts properly in accordance with the policy laid down by the Minister, the Minister must protect and defend him.

I come to the third category, which is different ... Where an official makes a mistake or causes some delay, but not on an important issue of policy and not where a claim to individual rights is seriously involved, the Minister acknowledges the mistake and he accepts the responsibility, although he is not personally involved. He states that he will take corrective action in the Department. I agree with the right hon. Gentleman that he would not, in those circumstances, expose the official to public criticism...

But when one comes to the fourth category, where action has been taken by a civil servant of which the Minister disapproves and has no prior knowledge, and the conduct of the official is reprehensible, then there is no obligation on the part of the Minister to endorse what he believes to be wrong, or to defend what are clearly shown to be errors of his officers. The Minister is not bound to defend action of which he did not know, or of which he disapproves. But of course, he remains constitutionally responsible to Parliament for the fact that something has gone wrong, and he alone can tell Parliament what has occurred and render an account of his stewardship. The fact that a Minister has to do that does not affect his power to control and discipline his staff. One could sum it up by saying that it is part of a Minister's responsibility to Parliament to take necessary action to ensure efficiency and the proper discharge of the duties of his Department. On that, only the Minister can decide what it is right and just to do, and he alone can hear all sides, including the defence.

It has been suggested in this debate, and has been canvassed in the Press, that there is another aspect which adds to our difficulties, and that is that today the work and the tasks of Government permeate so many spheres of our national life that it is impossible for the Minister to keep track of all these matters. I believe that that is a matter which can be dealt with by the instructions which the Minister gives in his Department. He can lay down standing instructions to see that his policy is carried out. He can lay down rules by which it is ensured that matters of importance, of difficulty or of political danger are brought to his attention. Thirdly, there is the control of this House, and it is one of the duties of his House to see that that control is always put into effect.''[285]

This analysis of the admittedly troublesome question of placing the doctrine of ministerial responsibility in a modern day context, where large Departments employ myriads of public servants, represents a judicious blend of adherence to fundamental constitutional principles and a practical recognition of the dangers of extending their applications to circumstances over which no Minister, however dedicated, could be expected to exercise the control that derives from his portfolio. What must not be lost sight of is the equally practical expectation that Ministers must govern and they are called upon to lay down and to enforce standing instructions within their respective Departments whereby "matters of importance, of difficulty or of political danger are brought to [their] attention". There is no suggestion in the Home Secretary's exposition of the modern constitutional conventions governing ministerial responsibility that it behoves a minister to build around himself a wall of ignorance behind which he can shelter when called to account by the House of Commons. On the contrary, all Ministers are put on notice that Parliament has the right and duty to see to it that each Minister in charge of a Government Department directs his attention, on assuming office, to instituting a system of administrative procedures that will enable him to be kept regularly informed on departmental actions that have the potential for public criticism, on methods that are open to serious questioning in terms of human and social values, and especially policies that have innate, questionable qualities which, when they surface, will expose the Minister to the heat of Parliamentary and public criticism. Where it is shown that no preventive action by the Minister could have avoided what has gone wrong it would be destructive of political responsibility to exact the price of resignation from the Minister concerned. Where, on the other hand, the negligence of the Minister is apparent in his failure to institute the administrative machinery that will enable him to exercise his ultimate responsibility for the working of his Department or those agencies over which he has statutory powers of control, the price to be paid for such deficiencies *may* well involve the supreme sanction of resignation. It is for the Prime Minister or, if the circumstances dictate, the House of Commons to wield the necessary pressures, and the Minister's parliamentary colleagues to judge the appropriateness of demanding the final sacrifice.

In considering the obligations of a Minister to respond to questions addressed to him by Opposition or Government backbench members it should not be forgotten that the basic principle of ministerial responsibility is to define it co-terminously with the duties and powers of the particular portfolio, especially if their source lies outside the language of express statutory provisions. This applies especially to those Ministers who continue to derive part of their authority from the prerogative powers of the Crown or governmental conventions. Where, however, Parliament has intervened and set the legal boundaries of a Minister's sphere of control the convention has grown in British parliamentary procedure to take a narrow view of the ordinary M.P.'s right to table questions that pertain to the day to day administration of nationalised industries, Crown corporations, local government bodies and a whole host of other matters that are helpfully listed in an appendix to the Report from the Select Committee on Parliamentary Questions in July 1972.[286] Among the recommendations of the same Committee was the desirability, on the part of both the Government and the House of Commons, of undertaking a regular revision of the classes of Questions which Ministers were not expected to answer.[287] What obtains in Westminster need not necessarily apply in Ottawa and we can postpone until the next chapter the position taken by the Speaker of the Canadian House of Commons in response to Opposition demands for answers to questions addressed to the Prime Minister and the Solicitor General arising out of allegations concerning the R.C.M.P.

Before leaving this review of the doctrine of ministerial responsibility it is necessary to advert once more to the special position which the Attorney General occupies in the exercise of his prosecutorial discretionary powers. Stress has been laid, earlier in this study, on the absolute necessity of isolating the making of decisions in this area of the Attorney General's powers from any direction that might be exercised on the part of the Prime Minister, any or all of the members of the Cabinet, or even Parliament itself. What then, it might be argued, does the acceptance of this principle do to the concept of collective responsibility as described in the preceding pages of this chapter? Is it acceptable to the Attorney General's ministerial colleagues in the Cabinet (using the Canadian and not the British model of Cabinet membership) that decisions which are capable of triggering high visibility political repercussions, which may seal the fate of the entire Administration, should be made unilaterally by one of their members, and at the same time expect the Government as a whole to bear collective responsibility? In answering this question it matters less that the Attorney General has consulted with his ministerial colleagues, either on his own initiative or that of his fellow members in the Cabinet, than the recognition that the ultimate decision as to prosecution rests in the personal hands of the First Law Officer of the Crown. Inherent in the latter principle are two related propositions, first, the Attorney General is saddled with *personal* responsibility for the decisions that he makes or which are made on his behalf under delegated authority, and, secondly, the doctrine of *collective* responsibility should not be invoked to involve the Government as a whole with respect to decisions pertaining to criminal prosecutions.

It might be persuasively argued, of course, that there are many other aspects of ministerial decision-making that call for the same degree of impartiality and objectivity that is claimed for prosecutorial decisions by the Attorney General and his agents. In the preceding chapter a full examination was carried out of the constitutional position with respect to the Royal prerogative of mercy. In Britain, as we have seen, that responsibility is claimed exclusively by the Home Secretary. Before formally advising the Sovereign the Secretary of State for Home Affairs might well deem it advisable to consult with some of his ministerial colleagues whose departmental interests might be involved, including the Attorney General on matters of law, but the final decision is that of the Home Secretary alone. It will be recalled that the Canadian system is markedly different from the British practice in these matters in that the decisions are made by the Governor in Council, i.e., by the Cabinet who can, if persuaded to the contrary, reject the recommendations of the Solicitor General as the Minister primarily responsible for reviewing applications for pardons.

Other examples that spring to mind are decisions governing the immigration and deportation of aliens, the compulsory purchase of a piece of property, designating the site of a new town or rezoning within an existing municipality, and the grant or revocation of a licence to engage in some form of commercial activity. Each of these may require the exercise by the responsible Minister of a quasi-judicial function, as to which he may be held accountable by the courts in accordance with carefully defined criteria that are associated with administrative and quasi-judicial powers. For a Minister to abrogate this kind of statutory duty in favour of the involvement by his fellow Ministers in the actual resolution of the statutory discretion, if brought to the attention of the reviewing court, would surely be regarded as unacceptable.[288] So far as I am aware, this important question has never been raised before the courts and, if it were, there would be some obvious difficulties to overcome in establishing the nature and extent of the Cabinet deliberations.[289] On the other hand, consultation with other ministerial colleagues could be equated with internal discussions within a Department in which perforce the Minister seeks the advice and opinions of his senior officials. Circumstances will also arise in which the statutory power vested in a Minister is exercised by departmental officials acting as the *alter ego* of the Minister. Of the illustrations quoted above, it is generally regarded as incumbent upon the responsible Minister to address his mind personally to questions affecting the liberty of the subject, so that a deportation order or a permit to enter the country would require the personal attention of the Minister. In other cases, responsible officials of the appropriate Department usually make the decisions.[290] Whichever of these conditions prevails, the Minister's responsibility is personal not collective in character, and it should make no difference whether his accountability is to be adjudged in the courts or in Parliament.

A more difficult question would arise where the independent exercise of the Attorney General's discretion was perceived, rightly or wrongly, by the Prime Minister as casting doubt on the quality of the Law Officer's judgment. The proper place for questioning the Attorney General's judgment in a particular case is the House of Commons. That this forum and its equivalent in the provincial legislatures have shown themselves, in the past, to be lacklustre in the pursuit of questionable decisions by the Law Officers of the Crown is hardly open to denial. Neither is the observation that on such occasions a mood of party solidarity and partiality often pervades the debates. Unless, however, we are prepared to discard altogether the doctrine of ministerial accountability to Parliament it might be rather more profitable to seek ways and means of ensuring that our elected representatives achieve a better grasp of what is at stake in calling the Attorney General to explain and justify his actions at the bar of public opinion. Any move to dispense with the services of an Attorney General who, by virtue of his prosecutorial decisions, has lost the confidence of his caucus, his Cabinet colleagues or, even more importantly from the practical point of view, the Prime Minister, will almost certainly become a public issue. Moreover, as in the recent situation in Australia[291] where the Commonwealth Attorney General, Robert Ellicott, tendered his resignation on the grounds of what he regarded as improper pressures by his Cabinet colleagues with respect to the disposition of the private prosecution of the former Prime Minister, Gough Whitlam, and other former Ministers, it makes little difference whether the Attorney General's resignation is called for by the Prime Minister or is tendered on the initiative of the incumbent himself.

In the current state of public understanding of the constitutional principles involved in this kind of situation, it is readily acknowledged that acceptance by an Attorney General of the full import of the doctrine of personal responsibility for his actions may be the only effective instrument by which the special independence that attaches to the office of Attorney General in our system of government can be secured. To argue for the adoption of the contrary principle whereby the more sensitive questions affecting criminal prosecutions are accepted as a normal part of Cabinet deliberations, giving full rein to the introduction of extraneous factors including the political interests of the party in power, is to assail one of the central supporting arms of our independent courts. What is at stake is the quality of justice that society aspires to see achieved in its name, the same tenet by which the duties of the prescribing judge and the rules of evidence and procedure govern the conduct of a criminal trial. The thought of permitting the introduction of party political considerations into the trial of a criminal case is abhorrent and rejected out of hand. So, I would argue, should be the approach to permitting the Cabinet to become directly involved in the making of decisions governing the institution or withdrawal of criminal prosecutions. In short, the doctrine of collective ministerial responsibility should have no place in the machinery of prosecutions.

12. The responsibilities of the Prime Minister and the Solicitor General of Canada for the police and security service operations of the R.C.M.P.

The translation of British constitutional theory and practice into the Canadian setting is evidenced by the declaration in the preamble to the British North America Act, 1867, that Canada was to have "a constitution similar in principle to that of the United Kingdom". Surprisingly, the same statute provides scant elaboration of this evocative statement. The "executive government" of Canada, the B.N.A. Act pronounced, was vested in "the Queen"; the Governor General was to exercise the Queen's powers and the Queen's Privy Council for Canada was to be the repository of the "aid and advice" functions that theoretically explain the relationship between the elected representatives of the people and the Sovereign as the Head of State.[292] Totally inadequate as these brief propositions are to an understanding of responsible government, as Professor Peter Hogg explains in his recent treatise on the *Constitutional Law of Canada:*

> "The B.N.A. Act was drafted the way it was because the framers knew that the extensive powers reposed in the Queen and Governor General would be exercised in accordance with the conventions of responsible government, that is to say, under the advice (meaning direction) of the cabinet or in some cases the Prime Minister. Modern statutes continue this strange practice of ignoring the Prime Minister (or provincial Premier) and his cabinet. They always grant powers to the Governor General in Council (or the Lieutenant Governor in Council) when they intend to grant powers to the cabinet. The numerous statutes which do this are, of course, enacted in the certain knowledge that the conventions of responsible government will shift the effective power into the hands of the elected ministry where it belongs."[293]

The year 1867, we need hardly remind ourselves, was no watershed in the achievement of responsible government in Canada. That constitutional goal had been attained and practised in each of the uniting colonies for many years before the advent of Confederation. The first half of the nineteenth century had seen the gradual dismantling, in the provinces of Canada, Nova Scotia and New Brunswick, of the erstwhile system of colonial rule from London. At the heart of the new colonial arrangements was dedication to the principles of responsible government and ministerial responsibility. The rejection of direct colonial rule from Whitehall was coupled with the adoption within Canada of a replica of the British system of parliamentary government in Westminster.

The principal elements in this transposition from Britain to Canada of constitutional responsibility for the exercise of power have been developed more fully by Professor R. MacGregor Dawson in a notable essay on the Cabinet,[294] in which he makes some pointed observations that have a particular bearing on the questions facing the McDonald Commission of Inquiry. Thus, Dawson writes:[295]

> "The Cabinet is above everything else responsible to the House of Commons, not as individuals alone, but collectively as well. This responsibility has been the key to the control of the executive power in Canada as in Britain: the powers of the Crown have remained for the most part intact or have even been increased, but the exercise of those powers has come under the Cabinet, and this body in turn under the general scrutiny of Parliament. This is the central fact of parliamentary democracy: for it is this practice which keeps the system both efficient and constantly amenable to popular control. The Minister at the head of every department is held responsible for everything that is done within that department; and inasmuch as he will expect praise or assume blame for all the acts of his subordinates, he must have the final word in any important decision that is taken. Only if the Minister can clearly demonstrate his initial ignorance of the offending act and convince the House of the prompt and thorough manner in which he has attempted to remedy the abuse, can he hope to be absolved from censure.
>
> Closely allied to this and also both as cause and effect of the Cabinet's solidarity, is the custom that the entire Cabinet will normally accept responsibility for the acts of any of its members, so that the censure of one will become the censure of all. The members of the Cabinet therefore resign office simultaneously. It is not impossible, however, for the House to censure one member or to allow a Cabinet to throw an offending Minister to the wolves and to accept such drastic action as offering sufficient amends for wrong-doing, provided, of course, that the Cabinet clearly did not countenance the objectionable act and that the purge was made with promptitude and without equivocation. Such charity, however, can scarcely be expected, and it must depend on both the mitigating circumstances and on the way in which the House chooses to regard the whole incident."

This exposition of the Canadian way of doing things and of giving substance to the doctrine of individual ministerial responsibility must be examined in the light of the present climate of ministerial and parliamentary opinion. To remain viable, old dogmas need an injection from time to time of public adherence to the constitutional doctrines that are involved. Furthermore, such doctrines are sustainable only to the extent that there is universal, or nearly universal, acceptance of their implications. It would be idle to deny that there has been evidence in recent years suggestive of a dragging of ministerial feet when faced with revelations of wrongdoing or incompetence in the Department over which the Ministers concerned preside. Of these contemporary events the Lockheed affair of 1976 can be seen as illustrating dramatically the conflict between the traditional interpretation of ministerial responsibility, as exemplified in the passage just quoted from MacGregor Dawson's essay written in 1946, and the powers of resistance of a recalcitrant Minister, when outwardly supported by his Cabinet and caucus colleagues.[296]

In the course of the recent Commons debates upon the ministerial accountability of the Solicitor General of Canada and his obligation to answer questions that relate to the activities of the R.C.M.P., there have been several important pronouncements that must be placed alongside the doctrinal analyses of constitutional writers. Amongst these statements is the carefully considered reply by the Speaker to an exasperated Opposition that found itself being stonewalled by Solicitor General J.J. Blais in his stubborn refusal to answer questions about events that preceded his assumption of that particular office. The essence of the Speaker's position was that a distinction must be drawn between the "informational sense" of a Minister's responsibility to Parliament and the "direct administrative responsibility" of a Minister for the actions of his department.[297] Parliamentary practice has consistently adhered to the convention that former Ministers cannot be required to answer questions that pertain to their former portfolio, because to do so would mean that the responsibility of the present incumbent would only go back to the date of his appointment.[298] "If it turns out" the Speaker added "that the evidence discloses that a civil servant in the department has been somehow misinformed or has been guilty of misconduct, for which the Minister has to direct an apology to Parliament, surely the Minister cannot be called upon to resign. However, if it is during the period of time when that Minister has been in office, then either the civil servant is fired or the minister is disciplined."[299] In much the same language Prime Minister Trudeau acknowledged that "...the government as a whole is responsible for things which happen or things which do not happen during its term of office. A change of Cabinet Ministers from time to time does not allow the government to escape the duty and obligation of answering for its administration... The Solicitor General has to answer not only for his administration in the period during which he will be Solicitor General but he will answer to acts committed or not committed during the period in which this government has held office".[300] Clearly, the Prime Minister in the above passage was defining the limits of ministerial accountability in the informational sense only.

On the more controversial subject of how far, when dealing with the police, and the Royal Canadian Mounted Police in particular, the application of the doctrine of ministerial responsibility should be distinguished from that which pertains in the case of an ordinary department of Government, the former Prime Minister has repeatedly maintained that there is another fundamental distinction to be made. There is every indication that all his Cabinet colleagues and the entire government caucus took the same position. Basically the argument is as follows. In order to achieve the larger goal of impartiality in the enforcement of the criminal law and to manifest the absence of political interference with the police and the Security Service there should be the minimum amount of direction and control over all branches of the R.C.M.P. Alluding to the events surrounding the FLQ crisis in 1970 and to a series of meetings betwen the senior officers of the Security Service and the Cabinet, Mr. Trudeau informed the House of Commons that the R.C.M.P. were directed "to pay a little more attention to internal subversion caused by ideological sources in Canada and not only [to] concentrate on externally sponsored types of subversion".[301] The purpose of these meetings, the Prime Minister readily acknowledged, was to receive information from the Security Service and, in turn, to convey the desires and general directives of the Cabinet of the day. In this way the police in a sense could be controlled and have spelt out the areas with which they should be more particularly concerned.[302] It was in conformity with this philosophy that the now well known Cabinet directive of March 27, 1975 was issued.[303] Under the heading "The Role, Tasks and Methods of the R.C.M.P. Security Service", the Cabinet agreed that:

"a) the RCMP Security Service be authorized to maintain internal security by discerning, monitoring, investigating, deterring, preventing and countering individuals and groups in Canada when there are reasonable and probable grounds to believe that they may be engaged in or may be planning to engage in:

    i) espionage or sabotage;

    ii) foreign intelligence activities directed toward gathering intelligence information relating to Canada;

    iii) activities directed toward accomplishing governmental change within Canada or elsewhere by force or violence or any criminal means;

    iv) activities by a foreign power directed toward actual or potential attack or other hostile acts against Canada;

    v) activities of a foreign or domestic group directed toward the commission of terrorists acts in or against Canada; or

    vi) the use or the encouragement of the use of force, violence or any criminal means, or the creation or exploitation of civil disorder, for the purpose of accomplishing any of the activities referred to above;

b) the RCMP Security Service be required to report on its activities on an annual basis to the Cabinet Committee on Security and Intelligence;

c) the Solicitor General prepare for consideration by the Prime Minister a public statement concerning the role of the RCMP Security Service."

The circumstances preceding the issue of this central fiat must not be overlooked insomuch as the Cabinet was reacting to the disclosure that the Security Service branch of the R.C.M.P. had been systematically monitoring the Parti Quebecois, a legally constituted political party. This activity was not countenanced by the Prime Minister or his Cabinet colleagues. As soon as knowledge of its existence was drawn to their attention, Mr. Trudeau assured the House of Commons, strict instructions were issued to cease that particular line of surveillance.[304] The most recent allegations of the surveillance of candidates for political office at all levels of government,[305] it must be confessed, foster doubts as to whether the Security Service has been dictated by the ethos that what is not expressly forbidden in unmistakable language can be assumed to have been tacitly authorized.

As to what happened before the 1975 mandate the Prime Minister has informed the House of Commons that no previous set of guidelines to the Security Service have been discovered, and we must assume that none in fact existed. On the interpretation of the government's mandate Mr. Trudeau stated: "There was nothing in the guidelines, of course, authorizing any illegal act, nor do I believe the common law guidelines existing before the general mandate given to the R.C.M.P. security services under the R.C.M.P. Act has ever referred to the fact that the R.C.M.P. could commit any illegalities. It was not found necessary by my government, nor, I think, by any previous government, to indicate to the police that they could not act illegally".[306]

Without wishing to emphasize the comparison too strongly, we may remind ourselves of the passage in Lord Denning's Report in which is quoted Sir Findlater Stewart's interpretation in 1945 of the British Security Service's basic purpose. Having outlined the duties associated with the office of Director General of the Service, the report emphasized that the greatest latitude should be accorded the Head of the Service as to the means he uses and the direction in which he applies them "always provided he does not step outside the law".[307] We can, perhaps, confidently assume that any further directives to the Royal Canadian Mounted Police, especially in the execution of its Security Service mandate, will follow the example reflected in Sir Findlater Stewart's report.

What is less certain is the ambit of control and direction of the Security Service on the part of the Minister concerned, and by the Prime Minister and his Cabinet, that should be regarded as constitutionally acceptable in a democratic society such as we understand that concept to mean in Canada. A good starting point is the statement of principles contained in the speech of the Leader of the Opposition, Robert Stanfield, when the report of the [Mackenzie] Royal Commission on Security was tabled in 1969 in the House of Commons. Mr. Stanfield's views, it is significant to note, were implicitly endorsed in 1971 by the then Solicitor General, Mr. Jean-Pierre Goyer, when making the first public announcement of his decision to establish a Security and Research Planning Group within the Department of the Solicitor General of Canada.[308] "I am sure" declared Mr. Stanfield in 1969,

> "that members of parliament accept the necessity that much of the security operation is conducted outside our purview. What would be cause for grave concern would be any thought that much of the operation is beyond the ken of the ministry or the Prime Minister; that there are not ministers, elective and responsible members of government to whom the entire security operation is an open book, who have continuing access to everything that is going on in that area, and who give proper, responsible, political, civilian direction to the operation on a continuing basis. None of us would want to see a security operation in this country running under its own steam and answerable only to itself — a government, so to speak, within the government. The very decision as to what affects security and what does not, what must be secret and what public, is finally a matter of political decision and judgment. The effective supremacy of the civilian authority must never be compromised in this matter."[309]

Given the generality of the wording of this statement we should not be surprised to find different interpretations being accorded to its underlying principles, the Prime Minister especially being opposed to a literal application of the "open book" approach.[310] "We in this government" said Mr. Trudeau, "and I believe it was the case with previous governments, have removed ourselves from the day to day operations of the security services. Indeed, we have done it from the operations of the police on the criminal side. We just make sure that the general directives are those which issue from the government and the example of that kind of directive was given in the guidelines of March 1975."[311] Responding to Mr. Stanfield's censure of the government for its failure to check whether the R.C.M.P. was investigating a democratic political party the Prime Minister clarified a little his interpretation of how far ministerial control over the Security Service should properly extend. While accepting the propriety of the Cabinet's concern with the scope of its mandate to the

Security Service and the areas into which the R.C.M.P. were looking to protect the security of the country, Mr. Trudeau emphasized his determination, and that of his colleagues on the Cabinet Committee, not to know about the day to day operations of the security branch of the Force.[312]

Since this question strikes at the very heart of what the present Commission of Inquiry must concern itself with when the time comes to state its views on the boundaries of ministerial responsibility as it relates to the Solicitor General of Canada, and indeed to the Prime Minister, it may be helpful at this point to include the fairly extensive exposition of this problem by Mr. Trudeau in the course of a press conference on December 9, 1977.[313] It can fairly be said to epitomise Mr. Trudeau's philosophy. Furthermore, in none of his speeches or statements in the House of Commons has Mr. Trudeau developed his ideas so fully on this ill defined but crucial subject. Asked by a questioner just how ignorant does a minister have to be of what has taken place within his sphere of departmental responsibilities before the constitutional doctrine can be invoked, Mr. Trudeau replied as follows:

> "I have attempted to make it quite clear that the policy of this government, and I believe the previous governments in this country, has been that they... should be kept in ignorance of the day to day operations of the police force and even of the security force. I repeat that is not a view that is held by all democracies but it is our view and it is one we stand by. Therefore, in this particular case it is not a matter of pleading ignorance as an excuse. It is a matter of stating as a principle that the particular minister of the day should not have a right to know what the police are doing constantly in their investigative practices, what they are looking at, and what they are looking for, and the way in which they are doing it.

> Maybe there are some people in this country who think that that should be changed. I have argued the contrary. I have even some concern with the amendment now in the Official Secrets Act which permits the Solicitor General to know at least some aspect of the day to day operations, that of wiretapping. I am even uneasy about that but, as an exception, I can live with it."

> I would be much concerned if knowledge of that particular investigative operation by the security police were extended to all their operations and, indeed, if the Ministers were to know and therefore be held responsible for a lot of things taking place under the name of security or criminal investigation. That is our position. It is not one of pleading ignorance to defend the government. It is one of keeping the government's nose out of the operations of the police force at whatever level of government.

> On the criminal law side, the protections we have against abuse are not with the government. They are with the courts. The police can go out and investigate crimes, they can investigate various actions which may be contrary to the criminal laws of the country without authorization from the Minister and indeed without his knowledge.

> What protection do we have then that there won't be abuse by the police in that respect? We have the protection of the courts. If you want to break into somebody's house you get a warrant, a court decides if you have reasonable and probable cause to do it. If you break in without a warrant a citizen lays a charge and the police are found guilty. So this is the control on the criminal side, and indeed the ignorance, to which you make some ironic reference, is a matter of law. The police don't tell their political superiors about routine criminal investigations.

On the security side,... the principle has been that the police don't tell their political superiors about the day to day operations. But they do have to act under the general directions and guidelines laid down by the government of the day. In other words, the framework of the criminal law guides the policy of the police and on the criminal side the courts check their actions."[314]

In commenting on this exposition of the subject by Mr. Trudeau it must be said at the outset that there has been a marked consistency in the approach which he has taken when explaining the Government's position vis-à-vis the Royal Canadian Mounted Police. Inherent in that position is the conviction that the best interests of the State are served in protecting the independence of the police, at all levels and in every jurisdiction, to the maximum degree possible and consistent with the ultimate accountability of the Executive to Parliament, or the provincial legislatures, for all police operations. The latter branch of this basic proposition, though sometimes overlooked, is no less central to democratic government than the principle of civilian control over the armed services which no one would question. The police are not a law unto themselves, they must operate within the purview of elected governments responsible to legislative bodies composed of elected representatives. Considerable effort has been made in Canada, as in Britain, to create buffer mechanisms that will keep at bay any misguided attempts at interference with the making of police decisions in individual cases. Earlier we described these as quasi-judicial in character and noted that they basically include decisions as to the scope of police investigations, the choice between taking a person into custody or permitting a citizen to continue with his normal activities and, most importantly, the decision whether or not to charge a suspected person with a criminal offence.

In according this large measure of independence to police officers there is the corresponding expectation that the preponderance of members of every police force will consistently uphold the standards of integrity, impartiality and obedience to the law that are the justifications for the State's investing the police with the panoply of independence. Both propositions stand or fall together, they cannot be separated. This is certainly so in what the former Prime Minister has described as the criminal law side of police operations. It is argued by the Trudeau government that a distinction has to be drawn between governmental non-interference with the criminal law aspects of police work and limited government interference in setting forth general guidelines and directions for the security service operations of the R.C.M.P., the police force that is charged with these special responsibilities. The assumption contained in this separation of R.C.M.P. functions and the corresponding difference in the federal government's role cannot be allowed to go unchallenged, but for the moment let us concentrate our attention on the criminal law aspects of policing and the proper dimensions of ministerial supervision and accountability for these kinds of activities.

Mr. Trudeau, in his analysis, sought to ascribe the source of protection against police abuses on the criminal law side exclusively to the courts and not to the government. The confidence reposed in the judiciary's ability to control possible abuses, either in the making or *ex post facto*, is, as Mr. Trudeau rightly acknowledged, largely dependent on the private citizen taking the initiative by either laying an information or bringing a civil action against the police. Irrespective of the question of costs, there would not appear to be a strong tradition in Canada of invoking the civil courts as the most effective route to follow in curbing police transgressions. Neither is it sufficient to invoke the right of private prosecutions without acknowledging the statutory powers of the Crown, albeit in the person of a provincial Crown Attorney, to take over such private prosecutions and to determine whether to press forward with the case or to enter a stay of proceedings. In short, the realities of the situation significantly diminish the theoretical controls by the courts and the citizenry to which the Prime Minister alluded. These realities are precisely the reason why we have seen emerge in recent years a plethora of ombudsmen, assistant ombudsmen and quasi-ombudsmen, in the form of civilian review boards, who are charged, *inter alia*, with the task of investigating citizen complaints against the police and, if possible, effectuating remedial actions. There has, however, never been any suggestion that these ombudsmen or civilian review boards should be accorded the powers of supervision over the day to day operations of the police with respect to which the government disclaims it has any responsibilities. "It is a matter of stating as a principle" according to Mr. Trudeau "that the particular minister of the day should not have a right to know what the police are doing constantly in their investigative practices, what they are looking at, what they are looking for, and the way in which they are doing it."

The weakness of this principle as the embodiment of the outer limits of ministerial responsibility for the police is that it treats knowledge and information as to police methods, police practices, even police targets, as necessarily synonymous with improper interference with the day to day operations of a force. This might well be the danger point that is perceived by politicians, chiefs of police and police governing bodies alike and it would be highly irresponsible to ignore the warning signals.[315] Earlier in this study I drew attention to the parallel that was drawn by the British Royal Commission on the Police between the independence conferred upon the Attorney General of England and Wales in the field of criminal prosecutions, notwithstanding the fact that he is a member of the Government, and the expectation that the Home Secretary, were he to be placed in charge of all the police forces in Britain, would conceive of his role on the police side of the administration of justice in like fashion. As the Royal Commission rightly perceived, the immediate safeguard against any dereliction from the standards of independence and non-partisanship that would be expected from both the Attorney General and the Home Secretary lies in the hands of the House of Commons and the vigilance of M.P.'s in calling the responsible Minister to account for his actions, on the floor of the Commons. By adopting British usage and the traditions associated with the office of Attorney General, the Parliament of Canada and the Legislatures of the provinces have manifested their expectations that our Attorneys General will likewise discharge their ministerial duties with sedulous disregard for all considerations of a partisan political nature. It is my contention that the Canadian public has just as much right to expect a similar non-partisan approach to the portfolio of the Solicitor General of Canada when this is directed towards police matters and especially in those quasi-judicial areas that fall within the criminal law side of R.C.M.P. operations. This expectation will not happen overnight but it can begin with a clear articulation of what is constitutionally expected of the Minister responsible for the police, whether it be the Solicitor General of Canada or his provincial counterparts.

Any contemplation of interference with police decision making should automatically sound an alarm in the mind of the responsible Minister. So much seems reasonably clear. This, however, is too broad a proposition to advance without qualifications of any sort. Elsewhere, when speaking of police forces other than the Royal Canadian Mounted Police, I have argued that undue restraint on the part of the responsible Minister in seeking information as to police methods and procedures can be as much a fault as undue interference in the work of police governing bodies and individual chiefs of police.[316] There have been occasions when the police chief of a particular city or municipality has been impervious to requests for information made by the member of the Government responsible for policing in the province. To my mind this attitude is unacceptable and is in direct violation of the ultimate accountability of the police and police governing bodies at all levels to the legislative assemblies of this country. The same is equally true of the Royal Canadian Mounted Police and the stance which the Solicitor General of Canada should adopt.

Because there has been so little examination of the implications of the alternative approaches we find ourselves faced with the dogmatic assertion by the former Prime Minister, echoing views of his predecessors in office, that interference of any kind with the day to day operations of the police is to be repudiated without question. Where no evidence is brought to light of dubious police methods it is natural that the principle of non-interference remains sacrosanct. The trust accorded to police policies and command structures serves to fortify the principle of non-interference. It is where the scenario suddenly changes and serious doubts are entertained, for example, about the ethos of police investigative practices that questions have to be asked as to what machinery does the state have at its disposal not only to take corrective measures but to prevent a repetition of the faults that are publicly exposed?

This is the question that must be borne in mind when considering the steps instituted by the present Commissioner of the RCMP to ensure greater control of Security Service operations. These administrative changes, instituted in March 1977, deserve to be set forth *in extenso* and are as follows:

"1. All new operational policy will receive the approval of a committee comprised of the Commissioner, the Deputy Commissioners and the Director General, Security Service before it is put into effect. In addition, all present policy instructions are currently under detailed review and where necessary, changes will be made.

2. The Security Service Operational Priorities Review Committee, which is designed to review and assess ongoing and freshly initiated operational projects, will be strengthened by the addition of two members, one of whom is a lawyer seconded from the Department of Justice, and the other, a senior officer with current criminal operations responsibility.

3. An operational audit unit is being formed with authority to examine all Security Service operations on an ongoing basis. This unit will report to the Commissioner. Formal audit reports will be provided on a regular basis to the Solicitor General by the Commissioner."[317]

Addressing the House of Commons Justice and Legal Affairs Committee on November 29, 1977, when the first public announcement was made regarding the above administrative reforms, the then Solicitor General, Mr. Francis Fox, emphasized the fact that the Operational Priorities Review Committee had the responsibility for ensuring "that the new operations are not only within the mandate given to the Security Service by the government but also within the law. It also has the mandate of reviewing operations that have gone on in the previous year to ensure once again that they come within the mandate and are within the framework of the law."[318] The Minister pointed to the seconding of a Department of Justice lawyer to the membership of the Committee as a major contribution to this end. It was with understandable surprise, therefore, that the McDonald Commission of Inquiry learned on July 6, 1979[319] that the written instructions to the Review Committee, issued in March 1977 by the Commissioner of the RCMP, omitted any reference to the examination of Security Service operations to determine their legality. Furthermore, it would appear from public testimony before the Commission of Inquiry that the attention of the then Solicitor General was not drawn to the significantly inaccurate statement that he had made when giving evidence before the Justice and Legal Affairs Committee on November 29, 1977, as quoted above.[320]

It is my understanding that in late 1979 new terms of reference for the Review Committee were placed before the Commissioner for his approval. These latest instructions expressly require the Committee to have regard to the lawfulness of Security Service operations.[321] Even so, distinct limits are set as to the kind of operations that will be subject to legal scrutiny. These limits include confining the review to past operations except in the case of newly identified groups or individuals who, for the first time, become operational "targets" for the Security Service.[322] An objective assessment of these "internal audit" procedures, set within the federal police force itself, might pardonably conclude that whilst the safeguards are a move in the right direction they ought not to be regarded as the sole protection of society against a repetition of past misdeeds. As to what additional internal and external controls might be considered I shall have more to say later.

In this connection it is useful to note the actions taken in the United States in recent years with the avowed aim of establishing effective and long overdue control over the Federal Bureau of Investigation. The initiative in this major exercise was taken in 1976 by Edward H. Levi, then Attorney General of the United States, as a result of which administrative guidelines were formulated to provide for ongoing review of the investigative techniques used by the F.B.I. in such areas as the use of police informants, police surveillance of suspects, the gathering of domestic security intelligence, and the dissemination of the information obtained thereby.[323] The monitoring of these activities is delegated to lawyers in the Office of Professional Responsibility within the Justice Department, an office created in the wake of the Watergate revelations.[324] The

Attorney General is only alerted if there appears to be a questionable practice involved, either on grounds of illegality or in terms of ethical standards, but the veto power of the Attorney General is unequivocally asserted.[325]

A similar role is conferred upon the Attorney General with respect to the counter-intelligence activities of the Central Intelligence Agency within the United States. Thus, under the provisions of Presidential Executive Order 12036 of January 24, 1978 the Attorney General of the United States is empowered to establish procedures to "ensure compliance with law, protect constitutional rights and privacy, and ensure that any intelligence activity within the United States or directed against any United States person is conducted by the least intrusive means possible. The procedures shall also ensure that any use, dissemination and storage of information about United States persons acquired through intelligence activities is limited to that necessary to achieve lawful government purposes."[326] The same Presidential Executive Order requires the Attorney General to report to the House of Representatives Permanent Select Committee on Intelligence and the Senate Select Committee on Intelligence "information relating to intelligence activities that are illegal or improper and corrective actions that are taken or planned."[327]

Despite considerable activity on the part of several Congressional Committees and political leaders there is no immediate prospect of charter legislation that would place on the Statute Book comprehensive measures regulating the activities of the F.B.I. and the C.I.A. and incorporating what is now regulated by executive and administrative decrees.[328] Not unexpectedly, there are signs of growing concern that the pendulum of control may have swung too far and that sight should not be lost of the nation's vulnerability if its government does not have available to it a sufficient level of reliable intelligence. The striking of a proper balance between these conflicting goals is a constant challenge to both governments and its citizens.

What has been established is the obligation on the part of the Director of the Federal Bureau of Investigation to provide the member of the Executive branch, to whom he is responsible, with regular reports of the Bureau's practices and procedures. How successful this new policy has been to date is a matter on which the McDonald Commission of Inquiry may wish to seek further elucidation. What is pertinent to the Canadian scene is the acceptance by a police force, that in many respects parallels the R.C.M.P., of its obligations to explain and defend its criminal investigative practices without thereby jeopardizing its independence in determining "[who or] what they are looking at and [who or] what they are looking for". In other words, the targets of police investigation and possible apprehensions should normally be left to the judgment of the police acting independently of the government. Any departure from this norm by the Minister, whether it be the Solicitor General of Canada or the provincial Minister of Justice or Solicitor General, would require proof of extraordinary circumstances to justify the action taken. In this kind of situation the tribunal that will sit in judgment is the legislative assembly and the wider public which, if it has the will to insist on the highest constitutional standards of ministerial conduct, can imbue government ministers with the right approach to take.

It is conceived, on the other hand, that the *methods* used by a police force in executing its criminal law mandate, "the way in which they are doing it" to borrow Mr. Trudeau's words, should be of continuing concern to the appropriate Minister and that he has not only the right but a duty to be kept sufficiently informed.[329] With information placed at his disposal the Minister must judge the acceptability of the police practices, not in his capacity as a partisan member of the Government but rather as an extension of the role historically associated with the office of Attorney General as guardian of the public interest. Governments having chosen to use the title of Solicitor General to describe the minister responsible for policing in the federal jurisdiction, and in some of the provinces, it is all the more necessary that the interpretation of the Solicitor General's duties be closely allied to those of the Attorney General. In exercising this kind of sensitive responsibilities we should be under no illusion that the Minister concerned can expect to be subjected to public and parliamentary criticism from diverse quarters. However, in the absence of effective controls over the police by the courts and an objection to resorting periodically to the cumbersome machinery of a Royal Commission, there has to be more immediate means of underlining the ultimate accountability of all police forces to the legislative arm of government.

Recent experience in the Parliament of Canada has served to demonstrate fairly convincingly the innate weaknesses of the traditional committee system in scrutinising the policies and practices of the Government in power. If the Public Accounts Committee is regarded as an exception to the general rule it may well be explained by virtue of its special composition, powers and the inestimable resource available to the Committee in the person of the Auditor General and his staff. In the area of ministerial powers with which this study is mainly concerned, involving the accountability of the Solicitor General of Canada for the R.C.M.P. and its Security Service, it can hardly be denied that the House of Commons Standing Committee on Justice and Legal Affairs has been a relatively ineffectual watchdog. Because of the "closed" nature of much of the Security Service's mandate and the amount of time it must take to acquire a sophisticated level of knowledge as to its operational methods and procedures, it may be asking too much of the members of a Standing Parliamentary Committee to devote sufficient attention to acquiring a thorough understanding of the subject that is crucial to exercising effective supervision. The large membership and changing composition of such Committees also are not conducive to the searching examination of witnesses who appear before them.[330]

What alternative machinery then should be considered to achieve that degree of public accountability for the Security Service which hitherto has been rendered immune from any study in depth, of the kind manifested by the present Commission of Inquiry. Consideration might well be given to the creation of a permanent Commission outside Parliament but responsible to Parliament. What is envisaged is not an executive but an advisory body composed of a small select group of individuals whose combined stature would command the confidence of the public at large as well as the professionals who comprise the R.C.M.P.'s Security Service. At first blush the ranks of

Canada's Privy Councillors would seem the natural source from which to staff the kind of Commission that is proposed, but it would be necessary to safeguard against a membership the preponderance of whose affiliations with any single political party would render the independence of the Commission suspect from the start. Preferably, the selection of its members would not be confined to ex-Ministers of the Crown or former senior members of the public service but would draw on the rich mosaic of all walks of life in which can be found the necessary qualities of experience, judgment, independence and probity.

It would be the Commission's responsibility to attain a thorough familiarity with the inner workings of the Security Service, its tasks and responsibilities, the R.C.M.P. and the machinery of government to enable it to express, where necessary, its judgment of any practices that transgress against the law or those ethical standards that should reflect the higher values of a democratic society. Such opinions, I would argue, should normally be channelled across the desk of the Minister responsible for the Security Service. In this way the Minister would be alerted to any operational or investigative practices that were judged to be of questionable legality. It would place him on notice that if he elected to take no action the independent Commission might consider what further alternatives were open to it to sound the necessary alarm. In exceptional circumstances the Prime Minister might be thought to be the proper recipient of the Commission's findings and recommendations. Furthermore, if the doctrine of ministerial accountability is to be reinforced, it is essential that the National Security Commission (or whatever other suitable name be accorded to the body described above), should have continuous and untrammelled access to the Justice and Legal Affairs Committee or such other Parliamentary Committee as might be made responsible for overseeing the Ministry of the Solicitor General, the R.C.M.P. and the Security Service. This might be by way of formal representations in open sessions or *in camera* briefings, with the expectation that the House of Commons should be brought into the picture if the circumstances warranted such a move.

There remains to be considered the assertion made by the former Prime Minister that a limited power of direction and control over the R.C.M.P.'s Security Service on the part of the Executive branch of government is inevitable and proper, but that this form of supervision should not extend to the right to know about day to day operations. It will be recalled that Mr. Trudeau expressed some concern about the exception to this principle contained in the recent amendment to the Official Secrets Act whereby the Solicitor General of Canada is empowered to issue warrants authorising the interception or seizure of any communication if he is satisfied on oath that such action is necessary for the prevention or detection of subversive activity or generally for the security of Canada. Despite his reservations about the Solicitor General becoming familiar with the specifics of this kind of activity Mr. Trudeau felt able to come to terms with the exception to the general principle. The basic philosophy remains intact and requires both the Minister, who is directly responsible for the Security Service Branch of the R.C.M.P., and the members of the Cabinet Committee on Security and Intelligence who exercise a coordinating function with respect to all the nation's security services, to keep their noses out of the run of the mill activities conducted in the name of Canada's national security. It is true that the Official Secrets Act requires the Solicitor General to table an annual report before Parliament giving details of the number of warrants issued under his signature, the average length of time for which the warrants were in force, a general description of the methods of interception or seizure and a general assessment of the importance of the machinery instituted under the Act.[331] A review of the reports tabled to date will readily confirm the suspicion that these annual reports are hardly calculated to enlighten M.P.s on how the system actually operates in practice, especially on the sensitive aspects of the minister's quasi-judicial discretion.

I have argued in this study that the Solicitor General of Canada and the provincial Ministers of Justice and Solicitors General, each of whom has responsibility to supervise the policing that is carried out within his own jurisdiction, should regard it as their duty to be kept informed of the methods and procedures followed by the federal, provincial and municipal police forces for whose actions they are, by statute, accountable to Parliament or the provincial Legislature. At the very least this should require the appropriate Minister to become familiar with each force's standing instructions on investigative and preventive procedures. Lest there be any misunderstanding, this does not entail an obligation to apprise the Minister of the daily operational activities of the police forces. What should not be left unresolved is either the persistent refusal of a police force to provide the responsible Minister with adequate information on matters that do not infringe upon the exercise of a police officer's quasi-judicial functions, or a persistent disavowal on the part of the Minister concerned to saddle himself with knowledge that is central to the fulfillment of his ministerial duties but which may prove difficult for him to defend in public.[332]

In what respect should the constitutional position of the Solicitor General of Canada be different when what is involved are the activities of the Security Service Branch of the R.C.M.P.? Several considerations need to be borne in mind. First of all, we should disabuse ourselves of the notion that the functions of the Security Service have nothing to do with the criminal law. Espionage, sabotage, terrorism, activities directed towards accomplishing governmental change within Canada by force or violence or any criminal means — all of which fall within the ambit of subversive activity as defined in the 1973 amendments to the Official Secrets Act — are just as much a part of the Criminal Code as crimes like rape, fraud, wilful damage and manslaughter. The difficulty is that the categories of subversive activity listed above stand alongside such nebulous items as foreign intelligence activities and hostile acts against Canada by a foreign power. Secondly, it is difficult to see where any theoretical or jurisdictional line can properly be drawn between, on the one hand, the criminal intelligence activities of the ordinary police, as part of the national police intelligence system, known as CPIC, for which the R.C.M.P. performs an overall coordinating responsibility and, on the other, the domestic intelligence gathering activities of the Security Service branch of the federal police force. It would be surprising if the body of data collected as part of these ongoing functions were to be divided neatly into two separate banks, with no cross access of any sort.

This having been said, it is also necessary not to overemphasize the common characteristics of the Security Service's activities and those of other law enforcement agencies. There is, for example, the real problem of deciding when and when not to invoke the normal processes of the criminal law including the bringing of charges for trial in the ordinary courts; it being well understood that resort, through the Department of External Affairs, to the *persona non grata* procedure for expelling a foreign diplomat from this country is often a more expeditious and satisfactory disposition of a case than the institution of a full scale prosecution. Another difficulty is the problem of determining how broad a mandate should be conferred upon the Security Service to gather intelligence and monitor the daily activities of subversive or potentially subversive elements that fall short of acts, attempts or conspiracies that are proscribed by the Criminal Code or some other criminal statute. As careful as we must be in understanding the special responsibilities of the Security Service, including its methods and investigative procedures, it is essential that we not confuse differences *in degree* with differences *in kind* between the execution of the Security Service's broad mandate, as described earlier, and the remarkably wide range of functions associated with a provincial or large metropolitan police force. It is precisely this confusion of thinking that is evident in some of the most crucial passages in the Report of the Mackenzie Commission in 1966 to which I shall refer in a moment.

The area of foreign intelligence gathering may well engender a whole series of related questions that must be faced if proper guidance is to be given to those public servants on to whose shoulders the federal government delegates the responsibility of protecting Canada's national security. Should there be, for example, different standards that apply in the pursuit of intelligence information in the possession of Canadian citizens and landed immigrants from that sought in the case of aliens and other foreign nationals? Again, does the location of the security services' activities have an important bearing on the approach that government should take towards the legality or illegality of such operations? In the absence of the kind of broader study that these questions pose, in which an examination would be carried out to determine the different standards that are incorporated into our laws pertaining to the rights and privileges of Canadian citizens and those which govern aliens and other foreign nationals or corporations, I will content myself with the following tentative propositions.[333] First, where what is being planned is the acquiring of internal security intelligence from Canadian nationals, albeit in areas that bear upon, or are in support of, the activities of a foreign power or foreign group, the same criteria should govern the Security Service's activities as those that apply to intelligence work on the criminal law side of both the R.C.M.P. and every other police force in the country. Secondly, if the intelligence target is a "foreign" target, involving a foreign national or agency, whether the target is located on foreign soil or within Canada itself, the authorization of such intelligence ventures would seem to be more a practical matter of exercising political judgment as to the likely international repercussions if discovered, than insisting upon a strict adherence to the domestic law of Canada or the foreign country. The possibility that a Canadian might be found to be implicated should not restrict the different approach that might be called for in the case of a foreign target.

Much the same kind of thinking appears to have been in the mind of Mr. Justice Hope, the Commissioner responsible for conducting recently a major study of Intelligence and Security in Australia, who observed in his Fourth Report: "With domestic activities, great care and judgment are necessary and legislative guidelines as to the nature of the activities to be guarded against are appropriate and advisable. The need for a balance between private right and public security provides a basis for the formulation of guidelines. With foreign activities care and judgment are also necessary, but the nature of the problems involved, the lack of any acceptable basis for formulating guidelines distinguishing one form of foreign attack from another, and above all the absence of a potential danger to democracy, make strict legislative guidelines neither appropriate nor necessary".[334]

I do not regard it as falling within my present brief to express any observations on the larger question as to whether the Security Service responsibilities should remain as an essential component of the federal police force. What does concern me is the view that security service functions are wholly distinct from criminal law functions and that, therefore, different standards and procedures are permissible. This approach, it will be recalled, was espoused by the Mackenzie Commission in their Report where it was argued that:

> "... there is a clear distinction between the operational work of a security service and that of a police force. A security service will inevitably be involved in actions that may contravene the spirit if not the letter of the law, and with clandestine and other activities which may sometimes seem to infringe on individual's rights; these are not appropriate police functions. Neither is it appropriate for a police force to be concerned with events or actions that are not crimes or suspected crimes, while a security service is often involved with such matters. Generally, in a period in which police forces are subject to some hostility, it would appear unwise either to add to the police burden by an association with security duties, or to make security duties more difficult by an association with the police function."[335]

I would argue the contrary and maintain that it is essential to inculcate throughout the Royal Canadian Mounted Police, including its officers assigned to security service duties, a firm adherence to a common philosophy wherein the line separating legitimate political dissent from subversive activity, admittedly difficult to define in theory, is constantly borne in mind, wherein coercive and investigative measures that are not sanctioned by law are not practised, and wherein there is a commitment to operating within the law instead of seeking means of surreptitiously circumventing its established provisions.

The final consideration that I would advance in support of the assimilation of constitutional principles governing the ministerial responsibility of the Solicitor General of Canada for both the security service and criminal law functions of the R.C.M.P. is the non-partisan nature of both kinds of activity.

Uppermost in the minds of every Cabinet Minister, including the Solicitor General, who has to address himself to questions affecting the security of Canada must be the public interest, the interests of the nation with all its diversities of composition and political outlooks. As I endeavoured to explain in an earlier chapter, it is in this sense also that political considerations are regarded as playing a legitimate role in the administration of criminal justice. Partisan motives of a kind that seek to sustain the government in power at any cost, to protect from the criminal process members and supporters of the ruling party, or to undermine the lawful aspirations of members of a rival political party must not be tolerated under any circumstances. This constitutional theory is now well recognised in the context of an Attorney General's prosecutorial discretion. Society has the right to expect that the same fundamental principles should govern the making of decisions at every level of policing and the security services up to and including the Solicitor General of Canada.

Of course, it will avail the Minister little if, notwithstanding his own commitment to the above interpretation of his ministerial responsibilities, the other members of the Cabinet, especially those who constitute the Cabinet Committee on Security and Intelligence, conceive the role of the Solicitor General in a different light. There is an obvious danger in stretching too far and too literally the parallel between the office of the Attorney General of Canada and that of the Solicitor General of Canada. It is true that the Cabinet has a collective responsibility for the exercise of federal powers relating to the Criminal Code, but this does not permit the Cabinet as a whole or any individual Cabinet Minister to issue directions to the Attorney General of Canada when performing his statutory or prerogative powers in the field of criminal prosecutions. As we have seen, this doctrine is in no way intended to discourage the Attorney General from seeking the advice of his Cabinet colleagues on his own initiative. Any failure to do so may well cost the incumbent his portfolio, though such a drastic step would likely itself be the subject of debate in the House of Commons in which public confidence in the Government would be at stake.

We have noted that in Britain neither the Prime Minister nor the Cabinet has a primary responsibility for the Security Service. It is, at the same time, well understood that the Head of the Security Service may approach the Prime Minister himself on "matters of supreme importance and delicacy". My understanding is that the same lines of communication prevail between the Director General of the Security Service Branch of the R.C.M.P. and the Prime Minister of Canada. Confirmation of this principle was forthcoming in the House of Commons on September 21, 1971, when the then Solicitor General stated:

> "I would also like to make the point that the Commissioner and the Director General of the R.C.M. Police Security Service, who normally report directly to me, also have the right of direct access to the Prime Minister in exceptional circumstances."[336]

Earlier, in 1969, the Mackenzie Royal Commission on Security had expressed the view that the Head of the proposed new Security Service "should certainly have the right of direct access to the Prime Minister when the occasion arises"[337] but with no elaboration of what would be appropriate occasions. Such uncertainty is undesirable and is calculated to generate unnecessary suspicion on the part of a Minister who finds himself being circumvented without his being aware of the governing ground rules. It may be helpful, therefore, to examine what might constitute "exceptional circumstances". It is suggested that these would arise, first, in a situation where, in the judgment of the Director General, either the incumbent Solicitor General or the Commissioner of the R.C.M.P. were personally involved in a case that called for investigation by the Security Service. Another category of "exceptional circumstances", it might be thought, would encompass situations in which there was an irreconcilable conflict of purpose between the Director General and either the Commissioner or the Minister concerned. In the event that the "exceptional circumstances" involved the Solicitor General only it would obviously be politic for the Director General to associate himself with the Commissioner in making a direct approach to the Prime Minister. Should the Director General of the Security Service, however, feel impelled to by-pass both his administrative and political superiors he would need to demonstrate a cast-iron case in support of his move. The price to be exacted for any misjudgment on the part of the Director General, acting alone or in concert with the Commissioner, could well involve the penalty of dismissal from office, a sanction calculated to deter any rash or intemperate unilateral action of the kind being presently discussed. Another hypothetical situation that could be envisaged as justifying a direct resort by the Director General, with the support of the Commissioner of the R.C.M.P., to the Prime Minister for the latter's intervention, would occur in circumstances where the Solicitor General of Canada refused to grant his warrant under the Official Secrets Act for the interception or seizure of a specified communication and the R.C.M.P. senior officers had justifiable grounds for believing that the Minister's refusal was unwarranted because it was based on personal or party political grounds. Here again, the spectre of dismissal for a wrong move would exercise constraints on any precipitate approach to the office of the Prime Minister.

What is less clear is whether the coordinating role performed by the Cabinet Committee on Security and Intelligence includes authority to issue not only directives as to the *general scope* of the Security Service's mandate but, in addition, the power to intervene and direct the Solicitor General as to the *manner* in which he shall fulfill his supervisory duties as the Minister responsible for the Service. Given the inevitability of different departments of the Government such as National Defence, Immigration and External Affairs being directly involved in certain aspects of the Security Service's mandate, especially those involving the activities of foreign powers, foreign nationals and foreign intelligence agents, it is only realistic that those Ministers should participate on an equal basis with the Solicitor General in setting the guidelines and priorities that will govern the Security Service's response to the problems facing the state. The same proposition cannot be advanced with the same confidence where questions of domestic subversion arise for consideration. Having regard to the elasticity of the whole notion of subversion, and the temptations which can easily blur the line separating legitimate political concern from improper partisan bias, there needs to exist one Minister whose judgment in supervising the application of the general policies of the Administration to individual cases and individual circumstances must be exercised from a position of some independence from his political colleagues.

In my opinion, any convention or usage that would involve regarding the Solicitor General in these *individual* matters as the agent of the Cabinet, or the pertinent Cabinet Committee, would not be conducive to the maintenance of public confidence in the Security Service. In arguing for the assimilation of the constitutional roles associated with the offices of the Attorney General and the Solicitor General of Canada, in their respective fields of authority, I am not blind to the fact that there are many duties connected with both ministers that call for the exercise of political judgment in the same way that their other ministerial colleagues in the Government administer their particular Departments. Clear examples involve the allocation of financial resources and the setting of administrative priorities within the range of each minister's departmental concerns. What I have endeavoured to do in this study is to isolate those special areas of discretionary power that are of a quasi-judicial nature which extend from investigation (and intelligence gathering) to criminal prosecution and which demand that both the Attorney General and the Solicitor General assume a strictly non-party mantle when making these kinds of decisions. Both ministers may pay heed to the broadest spectrum of considerations that relate to the public interest including, if necessary, seeking the advice and opinions of their governmental colleagues. When the final decision has to be made in individual cases, however, it behoves each minister to exemplify those independent qualities that alone can demonstrate to public satisfaction the absence of political bias in the operations of the police and security service branches of the R.C.M.P.

Notable support for this approach is to be found in the Report of the Australian Royal Commission on Intelligence and Security which reported to the Commonwealth Government in 1978. Speaking of the relationship between the Minister responsible for the Security and Intelligence organisation and the Director General of the Service, Mr. Justice Hope, the sole Commissioner, stressed the importance of ensuring that any act of direction or control, and any comment or suggestion made by the Minister, should be based on national rather than partisan considerations. It so happens that the Minister primarily answerable for the Australian Security and Intelligence organisation (ASIO) is the Commonwealth Attorney General, as to whom the Hope Report states:

> "In respect of matters such as the issuing of warrants, the Minister will obviously be required to adopt an entirely non-partisan approach, an approach which, as Attorney General, he has to adopt in many of his other ministerial functions. *And although it may be for other reasons, it is this type of approach he will have to adopt generally in his actions concerning ASIO.*
>
> He must therefore know enough about its activities to fulfill his responsibility to the Parliament. He must be ready to provide, and sometimes to offer, advice and guidance. He must be ready, when appropriate, to speak for the organization. But he must not become involved in the details of intelligence

operations or administration unless his duties so require, and *he must keep himself sufficiently apart from the organization so that he can see to it that the interests of the public, both in their rights and in security, are adequately protected.*"[338] (my italics)

In some ways it is unfortunate — it is certainly confusing — that the title of the ministerial office within whose portfolio the Security Service happens to be placed is that of the Solicitor General (in Canada) and the Attorney General (in Australia). What is being argued for in this study is not dependent upon the Minister being the Solicitor General of Canada. The same arguments would apply, if, say, the Security Service were to be returned within the ambit of the Minister of Justice portfolio (as it was before 1966) or if the Department of the Solicitor General were to be redesignated as the Ministry of Home Affairs. In England, as already explained, it is the Home Office that most closely approximates the Department which is responsible for the functions — police, prisons and parole — encompassed by our Solicitor General's Department. Irrespective of the name of the Minister who oversees Canada's Security Service the message conveyed in this paper, and echoed in the Report of the Australian Royal Commission, stems from a deep concern to ensure that the proper constitutional principles are clearly set forth in the final report of this Commission of Inquiry, thereby ensuring an informed public debate on the issues and a better understanding of the proper relationship between Ministers, Commissioners of the R.C.M.P. and Directors General of the Security Service.

Mr. Justice Hope, in his report, does not address himself to the relationship between the Commonwealth Attorney General and the rest of the Australian Cabinet on matters affecting the security of the nation. Instead he concentrates on the relationship between the Attorney General and the Prime Minister. "General security policy" the Hope Report declares "is a matter for central government and hence for the head of the Government."[339] Again, there is the statement: "Whatever the relationship between the Attorney General and the organisation (and its Director General) is or should be it has always been accepted that matters of security policy are, so far as the Government is concerned, the responsibility of the Prime Minister."[340] In defining the kind of matters that would fall within "general security policy", and thus subject to direction by the Prime Minister of Australia, the Hope Report confines itself to "general targets and priorities, budgetting and coordination."[341]

Transferred to the Canadian context, what in Australia is regarded as falling within the prerogative of the Prime Minister is better described as being within the jurisdiction of the Cabinet Committee on Security and Intelligence, presided over by the Prime Minister. Ultimate recourse to the full Cabinet on security matters, of course, is always a possibility and nothing is intended to diminish or qualify the special powers inherent in the office of Prime Minister as the Chief Minister who appoints and can compel the resignation of any member of the Administration. With these comparative refinements in mind it seems to me that both the Hope Report and this study have reached the same conclusion, in which the areas of involvement and the principles governing the exercise of the respective spheres of responsibility are reconcilable. What must be demonstrated is that the Security Service, like the other branches of the

R.C.M.P., is immune to political bias and influence and dedicated to serving only the national interest. These ideals are attainable by example and tradition, not by any charter, no matter how admirably the right objectives are formulated. Nevertheless, it is a first step to establish the right principles and to secure acceptance of these as constitutional conventions that govern the various actors in their political and administrative roles.

Emerging problems in defining the modern role of the office of Attorney General in Commonwealth countries*

by Professor J. Ll. J. Edwards of the Faculty of
Law and Centre of Criminology, University of Toronto

Introduction

1. Most of the Commonwealth countries represented at this meeting of Ministers of Justice and Law Officers can draw on a wealth of experience to demonstrate how easily troublesome situations can arise in the administration of justice, criminal and civil, which, if mishandled, are capable of bringing a government to its knees. Nowhere, in modern times, has the cardinal doctrine requiring the manifestation of integrity and impartiality in the administration of criminal justice at all levels been more dramatically demonstrated than in the recent Watergate affair in the United States. The revelations of blatant interference with the machinery of justice by the then Attorney General, in conjunction with his close associates and eventually implicating the President of the United States, underlined in emphatic manner that to tamper with the impartial exercise of the constitutional powers entrusted to the office of the Attorney General is to strike at the very heart of a system dedicated to the rule of law. To allow party political considerations, in the narrowest sense of that term, to supervene in the objective exercise of prosecutorial discretion is to guarantee the rapid erosion of public confidence in the administration of criminal justice.

2. Regrettably, a true understanding of this vital and fundamental constitutional principle has not always been evident in either the older or the younger member countries of the Commonwealth. It is to be hoped that the discussion of this paper, and the candid sharing of experiences with respect to this aspect of the machinery of government, will help to reinforce an awareness of the fact that the ultimate responsibility for ensuring that the essential qualities of impartiality and integrity are maintained in the field of criminal prosecutions must be shared by politicians and public officials alike. Ministers of Justice, Ministers of Law, Attorneys and Solicitors General, Directors of Public Prosecutions and their staffs must be constantly sensitive to the interpretation that will be accorded to their decisions, however intractable and politically difficult these might be.

---

*Extracted from the *Minutes of Meeting and Memoranda,* Commonwealth Law Ministers meeting in Winnipeg, 1977 — Annex to LMM (77) 10.

3. One thing is becoming increasingly evident throughout the Commonwealth and this is the fact that the traditional role of the Attorney General as the guardian of the public interest is no longer uncritically accepted. The emergence in many Commonwealth countries of the office of Ombudsman, with its aura of non-political objectivity, has served to raise doubts in the public mind as to the ability of an Attorney General, who is a member of the Government, and often with a seat in the Cabinet, to manifest an independent stance in situations where the government is seen to be actively involved as an interested party. There is apparent in many Commonwealth jurisdictions a questioning of what should be the essential characteristics of the office of Attorney General. In the course of this widening debate attention will surely be directed towards the familiar arguments concerning the merits and demerits of constituting the Attorney General as a public servant in contrast to that of a governmental minister. Examples of the alternative systems, as I shall examine shortly, are readily available throughout the Commonwealth and there could be no better informed forum than this meeting of Law Ministers and Law Officers in which to assess the constitutional, political and legal experience with respect to this important question.

Accountability of the Attorney General for the exercise of his discretionary powers — is it to the Legislature alone or do the Courts have certain supervisory jurisdiction?

4. Another tenet, historically associated with the office of Attorney General in England and Wales and transposed to those other countries which have incorporated the office into their constitutional machinery, is the exclusively political accountability that exists wherein the exercise of the Law Officers' discretionary powers can be questioned and debated in public. Parliament and the Legislative Assembly, it has always been understood, are the proper forums in which to call for explanations of questionable decisions by the Attorney General or his agents. Even this hitherto sacrosanct principle has come in for vigorous attack in recent years on the part of some members of the judiciary in such countries as Cyprus, Canada and the United Kingdom. On the one hand, claims are heard to the effect that the courts' inherent jurisdiction to control any abuse of its process justifies the nullifying, in appropriate cases, of criminal proceedings instituted or maintained by the state at the behest of the Attorney General or his agents. Where elements of persecution appear on the face of the record there is a natural desire on the part of many judges to reflect their condemnation of such prosecutorial practices. In Canada, a growing number of superior and provincial courts have invoked the principle adumbrated by the House of Lords in *Connelly v. D.P.P.* [1964] A.C. 1254, and subsequently reinforced by some, though not all, of their Lordships in *R. v. Humphreys* [1976] 2 W.L.R. 857, to the effect that every criminal court has a right in its discretion to decline to hear proceedings on the ground that they are oppressive and an abuse of the process of the court. This extends to stopping a prosecution which on the facts creates injustice. The

adoption of this principle to strike down prosecutorial decisions by Crown Attorneys, the appointed agents of the provincial Attorneys General, has by no means been universally adopted by all Canadian judges, many of whom perceive the larger constitutional issues involved in a conflict between the executive and judicial branches of government. Canada's final appellate court, the Supreme Court of Canada, has yet to pronounce finally on the ambit of the courts' jurisdiction in situations where alleged abuse of prosecutorial discretion is involved.

5. In England, meanwhile, as illustrated by the Court of Appeal cases of *Attorney-General ex rel. McWhirter* v. *Independent Broadcasting Authority* [1973] Q.B. 629 and, more recently, *Gouriet* v. *Union of Post Office Workers* [1977] 2 W.L.R. 310, the principle has been advocated that it is open to the courts to compel the Attorney General to state his reasons for exercising his discretionary powers with a view to determining whether the court should override the Attorney General's decision in the particular circumstances. In both cases what was involved was the Attorney General's consent to proposed relator actions. Lord Denning, M.R., in *McWhirter's case*, expressed his views forthrightly in these words:

> "I am of opinion that, in the last resort, if the Attorney General refuses leave in a proper case, or improperly or unreasonably delays in giving leave, or his machinery works too slowly, then a member of the public who has a sufficient interest can himself apply to the court itself. He can apply for a declaration and, in a proper case, for an injunction, joining the Attorney General, if need be, as defendant."

Lawton, L. J. enunciated the same doctrine but its significance made no public impact at the time in view of the Attorney General's subsequent granting of leave to proceed. Within a few years the problem arose again in the now famous case of *Gouriet* v. *Union of Post Office Workers*, the facts of which are probably well known to everyone attending this meeting of Commonwealth Law Ministers. Subject to whatever position may be taken by the House of Lords on the remaining issues between the parties involved, it is now clear that neither Lawton, L. J. nor Ormrod, L. J. lent support to the extreme position adopted by Lord Denning M.R. Retreating somewhat from the position he had taken in *McWhirter*, Lawton, L. J. declared in *Gouriet*:

> "I accept that the courts have no jurisdiction over the discretion of the Attorney General as to when, and when not, he should seek to enforce the law having public consequences. The Courts cannot make him act if he does not wish to do so; nor can they as of right, call upon him to explain why he has not acted. In this case he was given an opportunity to explain but, as he was entitled to do, he did not. I accept, too, that on the cases binding on me this court cannot proceed in relation to the Attorney General's law enforcement function on the same basis as it has proceeded when ministers have been alleged to have acted in excess of powers."

Ormrod, L. J. likewise entertained no hesitation in answering the constitutional question whether the Attorney General is answerable to the court, or only to parliament, for the exercise of his discretionary powers. Unequivocally, Ormrod, L. J. stated:

> "The Attorney General's discretion is not subject to review by the court, he is not answerable to the court in this respect, and like everyone else, he cannot be com-

pelled to act as a plaintiff against his will. There is, therefore, no clash or conflict in this respect between Parliament and the court or between the court and the Attorney General."

By the same token it has to be recognised that, if the views of the Master of the Rolls had prevailed, a major constitutional conflict would have arisen and it behoves all the Commonwealth countries to recognise the full implications of a repetition of the *Gouriet* situation in which the issue of jurisdictional boundaries between the courts and the office of the Attorney General may arise and have to be resolved.

6. As I write this paper (June, 1977) the House of Lords has begun hearing the appeal by the English Attorney General in the *Gouriet* case. It centres on the remaining issues as to whether a private citizen, who cannot establish any special interest but only a general interest in seeing that the law is obeyed, is competent to by-pass the Attorney General's fiat and to bring proceedings for a declaration (with the right to an interim injunction pending the final determination of the question of a declaration), that, by its public character would impose a strong moral obligation on the Attorney General to abide by its terms and thus fetter his discretion in allowing or disallowing relator proceedings to be brought in his name. In answer to the obvious question why, having succeeded on the major constitutional issue in the Court of Appeal, he should now be appealing to the House of Lords on the outstanding points, the Attorney General put it neatly when he said: "The answer is that the Court of Appeal, having bolted the front door, have invented a back door route to the same destination".

7. The claims, voiced in some judicial quarters in Canada and the United Kingdom, for some form of supervisory authority by the courts with respect to the Attorney General's functions and powers are by no means universally shared by all members of the higher judiciary or in all countries of the Commonwealth. Nevertheless, there is no gainsaying the fact that such judicial decisions and utterances in recent years reflect an underlying dissatisfaction with certain aspects of the Attorney General's constitutional powers and responsibilities, not the least of these being a lack of confidence in the Legislature's determination to breathe life into its powers of holding the Attorney General accountable to it for the exercise of his substantial discretionary powers. A view widely held, not only in the United Kingdom where the matter has recently been given considerable public ventilation, is that if the doctrine of accountability to the Legislature is to continue to be recognised as one of the bedrocks on which rests the justification for protecting the independent exercise of the Attorney General's prosecutorial and other discretionary powers, then members of the Legislative Assembly must resist the temptation when questioning the ministerial Law Officer to make party political points with apparent disregard for the deeper principles involved. The exercise of his discretionary authority by the Attorney General must be challenged and probed vigorously but members of Parliament, of every party, must understand that in adjudicating on what has happened they, too, are being scrutinised to see if they are having regard to the protection of the impartial administration of justice or whether, as so often is feared, they are contributing to a degrading of the higher ideals in favour of more transitory political advantage.

Should there be joint or separate responsibility for the various aspects of the administration of justice?

8. Basically, seven inter-related areas of responsibility can usually be subsumed under the general heading of the administration of justice: (1) police and law enforcement; (2) the initiation and conduct of prosecutions; (3) the courts, including judicial appointments and the legal profession; (4) representation of the Government and the State before the courts and tribunals; (5) the penal system; (6) legal advice to the Government and governmental agencies; and (7) the drafting of legislation and law reform. The question that naturally arises is whether, in practical terms or as a matter of principle, it is desirable that these variegated and extensive responsibilities should come under one portfolio or be shared among separate Ministries. If the latter course is adopted, as it is in most Commonwealth countries, further questions arise as to how the responsibilities should be divided so as to minimize the possibility of a serious conflict of interest arising out of the functions assigned to any one Minister. Just under 10 years ago, with the assistance of the Ford Foundation, I was afforded the privilege of visiting many of the Commonwealth countries and having extended talks on the subject of their work with Law Ministers, Law Officers, and their senior public officials. It provided me with a rare conspectus of the varying approaches that have been adopted throughout the Commonwealth to administer justice within their respective countries. I still recall, with sincere appreciation, the frankness with which we examined together many of the same questions to which I advert in this paper.

9. Various solutions to this kind of question have been adopted ranging from the English system, in which the responsibilities are shared between three Ministers — the Lord Chancellor, the Attorney General and the Home Secretary — to the system prevailing at the federal level in Canada prior to 1966, in which most of these responsibilities resided ultimately in the Minister of Justice and Attorney General of Canada. As a result of a public inquiry which examined the incumbent Minister's failure to reconcile his powers in the initiation of federal prosecutions with his responsibilities as the Minister in charge of the Royal Canadian Mounted Police, the Department of the Solicitor General was established in 1966 to encompass the R.C.M.P., the penitentiaries and national parole services, areas previously dealt with by the Justice Minister. In other Commonwealth countries, e.g., federal Nigeria and, until very recently, New Zealand, all the responsibilities listed earlier, except those of police and law enforcement, are concentrated in the one Minister who holds the separate portfolios of Minister of Justice and Attorney General concurrently. In such situations, responsibility for the police and law enforcement is usually assigned to a Minister of Police, Minister of Internal Affairs or to the Prime Minister. The pattern of vesting control of the police and security forces in the Prime Minister, and sharing the remainder of the administration of justice duties between a Minister of Justice and an Attorney General is exemplified by many countries, e.g., Malta and Sri Lanka. And there are many precedents for assigning responsibility for the police and its investigative and crime prevention roles to the Attorney General, e.g. Cyprus, Zambia,

Kenya and the Commonwealth of Australia, with respect to the Australian Capital Territory. In view of the variety of solutions which have been adopted throughout the Commonwealth, it would seem that there is a good case for exchanging experiences in this regard and for ascertaining more precisely where conflicts of interest are most likely to arise within different models of the administration of justice, and how best they can be avoided or resolved.

The relationship between the conduct of investigations in criminal cases and the decision to prosecute — should they be completely separate?

10. This question, which is derived from the more general problem posed above, merits separate attention. Although frequently adverted to, it is rarely subjected to the kind of informed examination that a group of Commonwealth Law Ministers and their senior advisers can be expected to devote to this sensitive subject. Essentially, what is involved is the resolution of the age old conflict between responsibility for the machinery of criminal prosecutions — especially the decision whether or not to prosecute — and that which is involved in controlling the investigative and preventive functions of the law enforcement agencies and internal security forces. Repeatedly, during my Commonwealth talks, I was told by various Attorneys General and Directors of Public Prosecutions that the exercise of control over the investigation of alleged crimes required the guidance of a lawyer, more with the aim of guiding the investigation in such a manner that would ensure the case being properly presented in court than any intrinsic belief that control over all aspects of police activity should rest on the Attorney General's shoulders. There was evident a marked disinclination to rescue a case that has been mishandled by the police and a preference for acting as guide and mentor in the early stages of investigation.

11. I was, therefore, particularly interested to see the same comment being made recently by a senior member of the Office of Director of Public Prosecutions in England, a country which has long subscribed to a fairly rigid dividing line between the investigation and prosecution of crime. Mauritius would appear to have a special problem in this respect having inherited both the English and continental systems of criminal justice. In the provinces of Canada, the Crown Attorney or Crown Prosecutor has long exercised a supervisory relationship with the police in their investigative roles, though, it must be emphasised, this falls far short of the theory and practice associated with the office of District Attorney in the United States. Whether the conflict is seen as associated with the lower levels of the administration of justice or at the ministerial level, where responsibility for both the police and prosecutions are vested in the same Minister, perhaps the words of a recent Attorney General of Ontario sum up the problem as well as any when he said:

> "...it is a contradiction, an incongruity to have a Minister of Justice charged with the administration of justice, who is expected to rule or act with an even, impartial

116

attitude and to let no other attitude than impartiality, objectivity play a part, and to have him also with the other hand directing the investigating forces and the enforcement side which is necessary in the administration of justice."

12. Of course, the determination of where, in the enforcement of the criminal law, the police function should cease and that of the prosecutor take over, is a delicate question which in most countries is answered in practice by unstated practical conventions rather than the application of principles carefully enunciated. It can be said with confidence, however, that the manner in which the criminal law is administered in any given jurisdiction and the confidence it engenders among the general population will relate directly to the greatest degree of separation possible between the functions of these important criminal justice agencies.

The problem of securing independence from political influence in the control of prosecutions, whilst at the same time maintaining political accountability for the exercise of that control in individual cases.

13. What we are concerned with here is the question whether the control of the entire machinery of criminal prosecutions, namely, the initiation and the withdrawal of criminal proceedings, should be in the hands of a political Minister or Attorney General responsible to the Legislature, or be exercised by an independent, non political Director of Public Prosecutions who is a member of the public service. In either case, there are the accompanying problems as to what are the essential ingredients of independence and accountability and how can these basic constituent elements best be combined and protected.

14. A review of the existing systems operating at present throughout the Commonwealth produces a somewhat bewildering series of alternative arrangements, the nature of which cannot be fully understood without reference to the prevailing political context of each individual country, and that task is beyond the confines of the present discussion paper. Nevertheless, it may be helpful to identify below the respective models, most of which derive from express provisions in the country's constitution though this practice is not universally adopted, in which event resort must be had to other legislative sources to ascertain the precise formula that governs the exercise of prosecutorial functions.

Model No. 1
Where the Attorney General is a public servant, combines with his office the functions of a Director of Public Prosecutions and is not subject to the directions or control of any other person or authority.
Countries exemplifying this model include Kenya, Sierra Leone[1], Singapore, Pakistan, Sri Lanka, Malta, Cyprus, Western Samoa, Bahamas, Trinidad and Tobago[2], Botswana and Seychelles.

Model No. 2

The Attorney General is a political appointment. He is a member of the Government but, although holding ministerial office, he does not sit regularly as a member of the Cabinet.

Alone of all the Commonwealth countries, strangely enough, the Attorney General of England and Wales typifies this particular category. The reasons for his exclusion from the Cabinet, which date back to 1928, have been fully elaborated in my earlier study of *The Law Officers of the Crown* (1964).

Model No. 3

The Attorney General is a member of the Government and, as such, is normally included within the ranks of Cabinet Ministers. In some jurisdictions, though this is by no means a universal practice, the office of Attorney General is combined with the portfolio of Minister of Justice (or similar title).

Most of the Canadian provinces and the Federal Government have adopted this model. Other countries that fall within this category include Australia (both the States and the Commonwealth Government), Nigeria and Ghana.

Where, in these jurisdictions, there exists a Director of Public Prosecutions (or its equivalent as in Ontario where the office is designated Director of Crown Attorneys) the Director is, in the ultimate analysis, subject to the direction and control of the Attorney General. How frequently such direction is exercised is a separate study but worthy of attention in the context of explaining the theory and practice of individual countries.

Model No. 4

The Director of Public Prosecutions is a public servant, who is not subject to the direction or control of any other person or authority.

This model will be recognised as the classic Commonwealth Office pattern which the United Kingdom Government consistently sought to incorporate in the independence constitutions of many of the countries represented at the present meeting. Following independence, in many instances this particular provision was changed to bring the D.P.P. under the direct control of the Attorney General. Jamaica and Guyana, however, have retained the total independence of the office of Director of Public Prosecutions.

Model No. 5

The Director of Public Prosecutions is a public servant. In the exercise of his powers he is subject to the directions of the President but no other person.

This is the situation that exists in Tanzania and which prevailed in Ghana during the latter stage of the first Republic from 1962 to 1966.

Model No. 6

The Director of Public Prosecutions is a public servant. Generally, the D.P.P. is not subject to control by any other person but if, in his judgment, a case involves general considerations of public policy the Director of Public Prosecutions must bring the case to the attention of the Attorney General who is then enpowered to give directions to the Director.

This model is applicable in Zambia alone at present. In Malawi, it is of interest to note, the Director of Public Prosecutions is subject to the directions of the Attorney General. If however, the Attorney General is a public servant, the Minister responsible for the administration of justice may require any case, or class of cases, to be submitted to him for directions as to the institution or discontinuance of criminal proceedings.

15. An evaluation of these constitutional alternatives in the abstract, important as it undoubtedly may be in more than a theoretical sense, will prove to be an inadequate exercise if attention is not directed also to some concurrent factors. Thus, uppermost in the minds of those who place a high premium on safeguarding the independent exercise of prosecutorial decision-making is the vital necessity of resisting improper political pressure. I subscribe fully to this fundamental proposition but it is essential to clarify the precise meaning accorded to the term "politics" in this particular context, if misunderstandings are to be avoided and workable boundaries drawn between those political considerations to which it is proper for an Attorney General or Director of Public Prosecutions to have regard and those which never should be entertained. It is a depressing fact that in nearly all discussions on this central issue that I am familiar with, or have listened to, the term "politics" has been invoked as if it possessed only one connotation, usually harmful. In truth, there is a basic line of demarcation that needs to be understood by everyone connected with the administration of justice, practitioners and critics alike.

16. Thus, anything savouring of personal advancement or sympathy felt by an Attorney General towards a political colleague or which relates to the political fortunes of his party and the government in power should not be countenanced if adherence to the principles of impartiality and integrity are to be publicly manifested. This does not mean that the Attorney General or the Director of Public Prosecutions should not have regard to political considerations in the non-party political interpretation of the term "politics". For example the maintenance of harmonious international relations between states, the reduction of strife between ethnic groups, the maintenance of industrial peace, and generally the interests of the public at large are legitimate political group or factional interest. As I understand the term in the present proceedings and, an even more sensitive question, whether (or when) to discontinue a criminal prosecution. All these broad political considerations, whether domestic or international in character, must be seen to involve the wider public interest that benefits the population at large rather than any single political group or factional interest. As I understood the term in the present discussion, partisan politics has a much narrower focus and is designed to protect or advance the retention of constitutional power by the incumbent government and its political supporters. It is the intervention of political considerations in this latter sense of partisan politics that should have no place in the making of prosecutorial decisions by Directors of Public Prosecutions or Attorneys General.

17.   My researches have left me with the uncomfortable feeling that in all parts of the Commonwealth there is much more to be done before the fundamental nature of the principles enunciated above are fully recognised. My investigations, for example, in the West African countries of the Commonwealth lead me to conclude that in the years immediately following independence it was the exception rather than the rule for the Executive to dissociate itself from the process of decision making in the field of prosecutions. I had expected to find in the older countries of the Commonwealth a firm adherence to the constitutional doctrine accepted in England and Wales since the famous *Campbell* affair in 1924. It came, therefore, as a surprise to learn that in at least one state of Australia the Cabinet has for many years been accustomed to controlling the power, legally vested in the Attorney General, of entering a *nolle prosequi* in certain classes of criminal proceedings. Discussion by the Cabinet of the initiation and extent of criminal prosecutions, I was also informed, is a common occurrence in New Zealand,[3] while the rules for the conduct of legal affairs in the government of one of the Indian States go further and are quite explicit in laying down the Executive's final authority for the initiation and withdrawal of criminal prosecutions.

18.   The basic question, I suggest, is who should be the final arbiter of legitimate political considerations affecting prosecutions, the Cabinet, the Prime Minister or Chief Executive, or the Attorney General (or Director of Public Prosecutions if the constitution has made the office truly independent). In my view, it is not only proper but desirable that the Attorney General (or the D.P.P.) should exercise both legal judgment and an appropriate degree of political sensibilities when assessing the weight to be given to relevant political considerations of the legitimate kind to which I have referred earlier. Where matters of high state or the general public interest are involved it makes eminent sense for the Attorney General to consult his ministerial colleagues, including, if necessary, the Chief Executive, with a view to estimating their particular contributions to an understanding of the wider issues that may be involved. Hopefully, the occasions where such consultations become advisable will be few and far between. In any event, what must not be allowed to happen is an abdication by the Attorney General of his ultimate authority and responsibility for making the final decision. This may be thought to be counselling the ideal situation and I recognise how far short the actual practice may fall in fulfilling this kind of proper relationship. In my Commonwealth visits I was reminded again and again of how important harmonious relations between the Attorney General and the Director of Public Prosecutions of a state were to the effective functioning of a system dedicated to the ideals of independence and impartiality in matters of prosecution.

19.   Given a thorough understanding and respect for the above principles on the part of ministers, politicians, public servants and those who shape public opinion, there would be every reason to look with increased confidence to the sustaining of the essential qualities in each country's administration of justice. Regrettably, I cannot say that I have found such respect and understanding to be commonplace. The experience of both the older and newer members of the Commonwealth confirms my deep seated conviction that, no matter how

entrenched constitutional safeguards may be, in the final analysis it is the strength of character and personal integrity of the holder of the offices of Attorney General (or Solicitor General in some countries) and that of the Director of Public Prosecutions which is of paramount importance. Furthermore, such qualities are by no means associated exclusively with either the political or non-political nature of the office of the Attorney General. Instances of indefensible distortion of the Attorney General's powers can be documented in countries which have subscribed to the public servant model of that office, equally with the occupancy of the ministerial portfolios of Attorney General and Minister of Justice in other countries of the Commonwealth. It is these kinds of situations that induce general disillusionment with democratic government. For me it was heartening to hear the permanent officials of the Attorney General's Department in country after country expressing a firm acknowledgment of the great good which was in their power to contribute to the general welfare of society. This goal was seen to be possible only if there was adherence to the basic principle of maintaining independence and resisting partisan political pressures in the related areas of criminal law enforcement and prosecution. This lesson, unfortunately, is still far from being universally understood. I would earnestly hope that one result of my writing this discussion paper for the present meeting of Commonwealth Law Ministers and Law Officers is to underline some of the fundamental tenets of the office of Attorney General.

Recommendations

20. What further practical steps can be suggested to reinforce political, governmental and public understanding of the unique role of the Attorney General's office? I would like to advance the following for the consideration of the Commonwealth Law Ministers:

(1) Ministers of Law and Attorneys General should utilise appropriate opportunities to expound on the unique nature of the office of Attorney General and its constitutional role as guardian of the public interest.

If my assumption is correct that there exists throughout every country of the Commonwealth a vast body of public ignorance as to the essential role and functions of the office of Attorney General part of the blame for this state of affairs must rest with past and present holders of the portfolios and offices represented at this meeting. Reading the parliamentary debates, journals and newspapers of the respective Commonwealth countries evinces little of substance by way of public explanation of the office of Attorney General or its special responsibilities as the avowed guardian of the public interest. This situation needs to be rectified. In saying this, I hasten to acknowledge the efforts and example of those few incumbents who have done a great deal in this regard, and their positions of independence have been commensurately strengthened. Actions, it is often said, speak louder than words and I readily subscribe to this maxim. There remains, however, the ongoing task of educating all sections of society, not the least of these being the members of legislative assemblies and members of the legal profession, as to the powers and restraints that must constantly engage the Attorney General in making decisions that lie at the very heart of the administration of justice.

(2) A greater emphasis needs to be given in the curricula of law schools to studying the functions and powers of the offices of Attorney General and Director of Public Prosecutions.

Notwithstanding the central position occupied by the Attorney General's office in any form of constitutional government and the major responsibilities that the Attorney General's Department discharges in the broad field of justice administration, there is a singular absence of any serious attention given to this historic office in the curricula of the vast majority of law schools throughout the Commonwealth. It is little wonder then that the great mass of lawyers, past and present, lack the perception of the delicate tight-rope which the Attorney General of a country or province must walk between the adjacent fields of mainstream politics and independent, non-partisan judgments. Every encouragement should be given to Faculties of Law to introduce courses that are devoted to a better appreciation of the philosophy that should guide an Attorney General and the members of his departmental staff in the discharge of their manifold functions and responsibilities.

(3) Courses on law and the legal system need to be introduced into secondary school systems with a greater emphasis being given to explaining the foundations of law and legal systems and less concern being directed to imparting information about the minutiae of various branches of the law.

Within the older member countries of the Commonwealth it is a sad fact to record that among the vast population of school leavers, who will never advance to the university and possibly a legal education, the level of understanding concerning the foundations of the legal system and the administration of justice is disappointingly low in the extreme. This condition augurs poorly for the development of an alert and informed public, capable of speaking out when the incipient elements of a Watergate become public knowledge, or fortifying the stand taken by an Attorney General or a Director of Public Prosecutions in the face of political pressure or popular clamour that threatens the independence of these offices. To counteract this widespread vacuum in the educational progammes of our schools, steps should be taken to introduce carefully designed courses that explain to the young students the essential features of the legal system, the purposes of law and especially the criminal law which affects every citizen's life, the role of the courts, the underlying reasons for an independent judiciary and prosecutorial system and the nature of political accountability for the justice system. Some jurisdictions have begun to develop this kind of approach but it is a long way from being universally adopted and I should like to see Law Ministers taking the initiative to attain this important goal.

(4) Means should be provided whereby senior and promising staff members in Justice Ministries and Departments of the Attorney General can attend regional seminars to acquire a comparative knowledge of how other Commonwealth countries tackle similar problems in their special field of responsibility.

A common theme of my talks with Commonwealth Law Ministers and Attorneys General in the late 1960's was the difficulty they experienced in holding on to their able young staff members who invariably were drawn away to the more attractive fields of private practice. This reality will not readily change but I believe more can be done to strengthen the public spirit commitment that I found most encouraging in my discussions with the staff lawyers in the various Law Ministries and Departments of the Attorney General. Professional and moral support of the career public servant in the criminal justice system is a requirement that frequently gets neglected in favour of seemingly more pressing and immediate needs. And yet the neglect of nurturing this backbone may well induce greater problems in the future in terms of morale, self-respect and a commitment to the public interest of which we speak so often when discussing the overriding obligation of the Attorney General and his colleagues.

21. When, on the conclusion of my Commonwealth visits, I met with the Deputy Secretary General of the Commonwealth and the then Director of the newly created Legal Division, I indicated to them that my discussions had convinced me of the real need that existed to institute meetings on a continuing basis, among the Law Officers and their senior staff, regarding the whole subject of standards and the underlying philosophy which should govern the exercise of the powers vested in the office of Attorney General. It is a matter of great satisfaction that these meetings of Law Ministers and Law Officers have already established themselves as an integral part of the Commonwealth programme. There remains, however, the necessity for paralleling what has been done so well by the Commonwealth Secretariat in meeting the need for more experienced legal draftsmen by affording opportunities, perhaps on a regional basis to begin with, for the aspiring young state counsel to meet with their contemporaries and a few highly experienced Law Officers to discuss matters of mutual and contemporary concern. In short, I would urge the extension of the precedent being set at this meeting of Commonwealth Law Ministers, in including within its agenda an item devoted to the theory and philosophy of your respective offices, by affording opportunities for the permanent staff of Ministries of Justice and Law Officers' Departments to gain strength and commitment by drinking at the same well.

Footnotes:

1 The reference to Sierra Leone must be read in the light of the remarks made by the Attorney-General during discussion of the paper (see *Minutes of Meeting,* page 46).

2 The reference to Trinidad and Tobago must be read in the light of the remarks made by the Attorney-General and Minister for Legal Affairs during discussion of the paper (*ibid.* page 45).

3 The reference to New Zealand must be read in the light of the remarks made by the Minister of Justice during discussion of the paper (*ibid.* page 40).

Extracts from the Communiqué on the Meeting of Commonwealth Law Ministers, August 1977

''1.   The Meeting of Law Ministers of the Commonwealth which opened in Winnipeg, Manitoba, Canada, on 23 August with an inaugural address by the Chief Justice of Canada, the Rt. Hon. Bora Laskin, concluded on 26 August 1977.

The Meeting, attended by Law Ministers, Attorneys-General, other Law Officers, and officials from 30 countries, elected the Hon. Ron Basford, Minister of Justice and Attorney-General of Canada, as its Chairman.

• • •

Modern role of the Attorney-General

22.   Law Ministers discussed the great constitutional importance of the office of Attorney-General and the emerging problems of defining its modern role. In doing so, they noted that, although in the Commonwealth there was a variety of constitutional arrangements, the essential role was the same.

23.   In some countries the Attorney-General was a member of the Government and often of the Cabinet, sometimes also combining the portfolio of Minister responsible for Justice. In other countries the Attorney-General was a politically independent public servant. Responsibility for initiating criminal proceedings, often vested in the Attorney-General, was in some countries held by the Director of Public Prosecutions who may or may not be subject to the direction of the Attorney-General in the discharge of his prosecutorial powers.

24.   In recent years, both outside and within the Commonwealth, public attention has frequently focussed on the function of law enforcement. Ministers endorsed the principles already observed in their jurisdictions that the discretion in these matters should always be exercised in accordance with wide considerations of the public interest, and without regard to considerations of a party political nature, and that it should be free from any direction or control whatsoever. They considered, however, that the maintenance of these principles depended ultimately upon the unimpeachable integrity of the holder of the office whatever the precise constitutional arrangements in the State concerned.

25.   In order to dispel public misunderstanding in the matter, Ministers considered that practical measures might be taken by governments throughout the Commonwealth to improve political, governmental and general public awareness of the unique role of the Attorney-General's office.''

Footnotes

1. 1977 Meeting of Commonwealth Law Ministers, *Minutes of Meeting and Memoranda* (Commonwealth Secretariat, London), 195 at p. 203.

2. *Ibid.*, at p. 138.

3. H.C. Debates, Vol. 121, pp. 3881-3883, March 17, 1978.

4. Ontario Legislature Debates, Feb. 23, 1978, pp. 50-53.

5. See W.J. Eccles: *The Government of New France*, 1968, pp. 10-12, and Mason Wade: *The French Canadians* (1760-1967) Vol. 1, 1968, pp. 17-18. For an authoritative account of the Government of New France between 1627 and 1760 see Governor Carleton's Report upon the Laws and Courts of Judicature in the Province of Quebec (1769), which is published in full in W.P.M. Kennedy and G. Lanctot. *Reports on The Laws of Quebec 1767-1770*, see especially pp. 55-56.

6. See State Books of Upper Canada, Records of the Executive Council, Vols. B, C, E, and F, *passim.* Volume K contains a minute directing the Attorney General to forbear from prosecuting certain persons unless they were leaders of the 1838 revolt — see pp. 77-8, April 10, 1838.

7. 31 Vict., c.39, An Act Respecting the Department of Justice.

8. Bill 51, entitled "Offices of the Receiver General and Attorney General of Canada", was introduced in the House of Commons on March 18, 1878. The major debate on the Bill took place on April 2, 1878; see H.C. Debates Vol. 5, pp. 1584-1624, especially the well informed speech by Alexander Mackenzie, the Prime Minister, who reviewed the experience of New Zealand and the Australian colonies of South Victoria, [New] South Wales and South Australia in resolving the issue as to whether the Law Officers of the Crown should be political or public offices (at p. 1591).

9. *Ibid.*, pp. 1584-1590. Macdonald's parting shot, on the report stage of the Bill, was colourful: "You cannot have two chairmen. You cannot have a double-head. There is a three-headed cerberus; but there cannot be a double-headed Minister of Justice" (at p. 1624).

10. *Ibid.*, p. 1590. As Sir John A. Macdonald viewed the prospects, "The Solicitor General would be a handy man, always ready to go into the business" (*loc. cit.*).

11. The passage of Bill 42, to make provision for the appointment of a Solicitor General was effected on June 11, 1887; see H.C. Debates, Vol. I, p. 191, and Vol. 2, pp. 889 and 1121.

12. See H.C. Debates, Vol. 5, p. 1623, April 29, 1878; the attribution to Macdonald of the draftsmanship was made by R. Laflamme, the then Minister of Justice, and not denied.

13. See *post* p. 29 *et seq.*

14. See H.C. Debates, Vol. 5, pp. 1594-1595, April 2, 1878. The N.W.M.P. was formally constituted as a police force with responsibility for maintaining law and order on the western prairies under Order-in-Council no. 1134 dated August 30, 1873.

15. 36 Vict., c.35, s.11; and see Royal Northwest Mounted Police Act, 57-58 Vict., c.27, s.4.

16. 57-58 Vict., c.27, s.3.

17. 36 Vict., c.35, s.33. The Act, passed on May 23, 1873, did not establish the North West Mounted Police. Rather it was an enabling statute which gave the Macdonald Government authority to organise the new force by order-in-council when the circumstances dictated the necessity for such action. The final step was taken on August 30, 1873 under P.C. Order 1134. For a well documented account of the origins of the present federal police force see S.W. Horrall: "Sir John A. Macdonald and the Mounted Police Force for the Northwest Territories" (1972) 53 *Canadian Historical Review* 179-200.

18. Mr. Tupper in H.C. Debates, Vol. 5, p. 1594, April 2, 1878, refers to the transfer from Justice (when Macdonald was First Minister and Minister of Justice) to the Department of the Secretary of State. In the earliest stages of the formation of the North West Mounted Police there is considerable evidence that the Minister of the Interior was much involved in the organizational aspects of the fledgling force and in answering for the Government in the House of Commons. This, however, did not amount to assuming full ministerial responsibility for the North West Mounted Police — see S.W. Horrall *op. cit.*, pp. 193-195.

19. 7-8 Eliz. II, c.54, s.2.

20. 14-15 Eliz. II, c.25, s.4.

21. R.S.C. 1970, c.R-9, s.5. It is of interest to note that in the Australian Security Intelligence Organisation Bill of 1979, section 8 provides that the organisation shall be under the control of the Director General who is "subject to the general directions of the Minister [the Attorney General of the Commonwealth of Australia]". What is particularly significant is the further provision (s.8(2)) that the Minister is not empowered to override the opinion of the Director General:

> "(a) on the question whether the collection of intelligence by the Organization concerning a particular individual would, or would not, be justified by reason of its relevance to security;
>
> (b) on the question whether a communication of intelligence concerning a particular individual would be for a purpose relevant to security; or
>
> (c) concerning the nature of the advice that should be given by the Organization to a Minister, Department or authority of the Commonwealth."

I would hazard the opinion that the application of paragraph (b) above is calculated to give rise to serious problems, especially in the area of communicating raw intelligence information concerning Australian citizens to foreign intelligence organisations.

22. *Ibid.*

23. See *R.* v. *Hauser et al*, (1979) 8 C.R. (3d) 89, on appeal from the Alberta Supreme Court, Appellate Division, *Re Hauser* v. *The Queen* (1978) 37 C.C.C. (2d) 129. Shortly prior to the Hauser appeal, the Supreme Court had ruled against the constitutional validity of the Quebec Commission of Inquiry into actions of the R.C.M.P. in that province — see *Attorney General of Quebec and Keable* v. *Attorney General of Canada et al.* (1979) 43 C.C.C (2d) 49, on appeal from the Quebec Court of Appeal, (1978) 41 C.C.C. (2d) 452.

24. Effected by the Criminal Law Amendment Act, 1968-69, S.C.C. 38, s.2(2), in its amended form, reads as follows:

> "Attorney General" means the Attorney General or Solicitor General of a province in which proceedings to which this Act applies are taken and, with respect to
>
> (a) the Northwest Territories and the Yukon Territory, and
>
> (b) proceedings instituted at the instance of the Government of Canada and conducted by or on behalf of that Government in respect of a violation of or conspiracy to violate any Act of the Parliament of Canada or a regulation made thereunder other than this Act, means the Attorney General of Canada and, except for the purposes of subsections 505(4) and 507(3), includes the lawful deputy of the said Attorney General, Solicitor General and Attorney General of Canada;"

25. (1979) 8 C.R. (3d) at pp. 95-6.

26. The majority judgments were delivered by Spence J., and Pigeon J., (Martland, Ritchie and Beetz, J.J., concurring); Pratte J., concurred in the minority judgment prepared by Dickson J.

27. *Ibid.*, pp. 96-7.

28. *Ibid.*, p. 97.

29. *Ibid.*, p. 117.

30. *Ibid.*, p. 123.

31. In particular, reference should be made to the Ontario Court of Appeal decision in *R.* v. *Pelletier* (1974) 28 C.R.N.S. 129, 4 O.R. (2d) 677, 18 C.C.C. (2d) 516, leave to appeal against which decision was refused by the Supreme Court of Canada [1974] S.C.R.x, 4 O.R. (2d) 677 n. The judgment of the Court of Appeal was delivered by Estey, J.A. (as he then was).

32. (1978) 8 C.R. (3d) at pp. 126-7.

33. *Ibid.*, at p. 133.

33A. *Ibid.*, at p. 147.

34. H.C. Debates, Vol. 120, p. 3568, March 2, 1977. This statement should be contrasted with the same Minister's reply to a question on the subject of Henry Morgentaler, a Montreal doctor who had been acquitted on three separate occasions on charges of abortion. Referring to those circumstances Mr. Basford stated: "Whether people are prosecuted under the Criminal Code is a matter within the sole and exclusive jurisdiction, and responsibility, of provincial authorities and any intervention by me would be contrary to the relationships and responsibilities which exist under the Criminal Code and would be improper, as would have been any intervention by the province of Quebec with regard to the exercise of my jurisdiction in the matter of ordering a new trial" — H.C. Debates, Vol. I, p. 674, November 2, 1976.

35. H.C. Debates, Vol. II, p. 1302, November 27, 1969.

36. H.C. Debates, Vol. II, p. 1816, December 19, 1969.

37. H.C. Debates, Vol. I, p. 213, October 16, 1970; *ibid.*, Vol. I, p. 421, October 21, 1970; Vol. I, p. 546, October 26, 1970; Vol. I, p. 653, October 28, 1970.

38. See e.g., Solicitor General Fox's statement in H.C. Debates, Vol. 120, p. 7378, July 6, 1977. Compare the same Minister's reply to mail opening allegations, in H.C. Debates, Vol. 121, p. 737, November 9, 1977, saying that such complaints have not been automatically referred to the provincial attorneys general where the alleged events may have occurred. "I have consulted the Law Officers of the Crown and they tell me that the proper course to follow at the moment is to refer such allegations to the Royal Commission set up by the government last July." Some idea of the uncertainty that prevailed around this time as to what should be the correct policy is reflected in the Prime Minister's reply to a question by the Leader of the Opposition: "Each time an action was discovered which might have an aspect of illegality reference was made to the McDonald Commission... *and* to the Attorney General of the province in which the suspected action had been taken with a view to that Attorney General deciding under our laws whether a prosecution was warranted or not" — *op. cit.* p. 593, November 3, 1977.

39. See *post*, p. 38.

40. The authoritative decisions in Canadian law are *Rourke* (1977) 5 C.C.C. (2d) 129, *Osborn* [1969] 4 C.C.C. 185 and *Smythe* (1971) 3 C.C.C. (2d) 97, affmd., 3 C.C.C. (2d) 366. In English law, reference must be made to *Gouriet* v. *Union of Post Office Workers* [1977] 3 W.L.R. 300, reversing C.A. decision [1977] 2 W.L.R. 310, and the cases reviewed in Edwards, *Law Officers of the Crown* (1964), pp. 226-246, 286-295. For my comments on *Rourke* and *Gouriet* see the essay cited in footnote 138A *post* at pp. 381-388.

41. See, e.g., the letter from the Colonial Secretary to Maitland on November 10, 1823 instructing the Lieutenant Governor to direct the Attorney General to enter a *nolle prosequi* in the case of John Macdonald, who was indicted for high treason, representations having been made to the Foreign Secretary by the American Minister in London — see Colonial Office papers, G. series, Vol. 60. And see further the despatch of November 12, 1825 which suggests that the Colonial Secretary's "instructions" had not been carried out — *op. cit.* Vol. 61.

42. (1978) 39 C.C.C. (2d) 145.

43. *Ibid.*, at p. 154. My italics.

44. Statutes of Manitoba, 1885, c.5.

45. Revised Statutes of Manitoba, c.A 170, s.3.

46. Statutes of British Columbia, 1899, c.5. The wording remains practically unchanged in the Revised Statutes of B.C 1960, c.21.

47. Statutes of British Columbia, 1871, c.147.

48. Revised Statutes of Nova Scotia, 1900, c.10, s.3. No significant changes have been made in that province's Revised Statutes of 1967, see c.255, s.4.

49. Statutes of Saskatchewan, 1906, c.7, the terms of which statute are repeated unchanged in the Revised Statutes of the province in 1965, c.24.

50. Statutes of Alberta, 1906, c.6, and compare R.S.A. 1970, c.95 which repeats the terms of the earlier enactment.

51. Revised Statutes of Ontario, 1877, c.14, s.2.

52. Statutes of Ontario 1968-69, c.27, repeated in R.S.O. 1970, c.116.

53. Statutes of Quebec, 1965, c.16.

54. S.O. 1968-69, c.27, s.1. It is worth noting that Newfoundland, long before its entry into Confederation in 1949, had established a Department of Justice headed by the Minister of Justice who was *ex officio* His Majesty's Attorney General of Newfoundland — see Statutes of Newfoundland 1898, c.18. In 1949, the new province fell into line with the other members of Confederation and designated the old Department of Justice as the new Department of the Attorney General, see Statutes of Newfoundland 1949, c.49, s.9. Prompted by Quebec's example, Newfoundland in 1966 reverted to its original nomenclature and reestablished the Department of Justice with the duties of the Minister of Justice and the Attorney General being set forth separately, even though they are exercisable by the same minister — see *ibid.*, c.35.

55. *Ibid.*, s.5.

56. Government Reorganisation Act, 1972, S.O. 1972, c.1. Under the terms of the above statute, the Provincial Secretary for Justice is included within the list of portfolios that constitute the Executive Council but no mention of the duties attached to the new office is contained in the statute itself.

57. The enabling legislation is the same Government Reorganisation Act, 1972, that resulted from the report of the Committee on Government Productivity, see sections 93-99.

58. Department of the Solicitor General Act, S.A. 1973.

59. See Edwards, *op. cit.*, ch. 7.

60. See A.L. Burt in *The Old Province of Quebec*, 1933, Vol. II, pp. 40, 215 and Hilda Neatby: *The Administration of Justice under the Quebec Act*, 1937, pp. 339-340.

61. *Ante*, p. 7, footnote 9.

62. Solicitor General Act 1889, S.C., c.14, s.1.

63. See H.C. Debates, Vol. I, col. 3267, May 23, 1894.

64. In a brief historical excursus during the passage of the Government Organisation Bill, Richard Bell, formerly Parliamentary Secretary to the Minister of Justice, expressed the view that it was only Meighen's "parliamentary brilliance which caused the office to be raised to Cabinet rank". Since his incumbency only two Solicitors General, Guthrie and Fauteux, have held the office as a non-cabinet appointment — see H.C. Debates, Vol. V, p. 5521, May 25, 1966. The same speaker adverted to the lapse in filling the office between 1935 and 1945 "when two, strong dynamic men held the portfolio of Minister of Justice and Attorney General, Ernest Lapointe, and Louis St. Laurent, and the administration of justice did not noticeably suffer as a result of the vacancy" (*loc. cit.*).

65. See *Guide to Canadian Ministries since Confederation* (Public Archives of Canada, 1974) esp. pp. 53, 61, 67 and 75. Thus, to the exceptions noted by Richard Bell (n.*64 supra*) the name of Lucien Cannon (1925-26) should be added. All three exceptions at other times were given Cabinet rank as Solicitors General.

66. H.C. Debates, Vol. I, cols. 2063-2070, April 25, 1899.

67. *Ibid.*, col. 2069.

68. H.C. Debates, Vol. III, pp. 2892-3, March 11, 1954.

69. Order in Council P.C. 1959-1113, August 27, 1959.

70. And see the exchanges on the proposed abolition of the "semi-portfolio" of the Solicitor General in H.C. Debates, Vol. III, cols. 2221 and 2621, April 26, 1925 and Vol. V, col. 4628, June 22, 1925.

71. H.C. Debates, Vol. 5, p. 5078, May 19, 1961.

72. Vol. 2, *Supporting Services for Government*, Chap. 4.

73. Order-in-Council, P.C. 1965-2286, December 22, 1965.

74. See *ante* page 9 and footnotes 20, 21 and 22.

75. H.C. Debates, Vol. III, p. 2296, March 7, 1966.

76. *Op. cit.* p. 2297.

77. *Loc. cit.*

78. *Op. cit.*, Vol. I, pp. 4873-4, May 9, 1966.

79. H.C. Debates, Vol. V, p. 5524, May 25, 1966.

80. *Loc. cit.*

81. H.C. Debates, Vol. III, p. 1681, February 23, 1966.

82. *Op. cit.*, p. 1680.

83. Queen's Printer, June 1965, Catalogue No. Z1 — 1964/2. The report contains a series of extracts from the House of Commons Debates which triggered the convening of the inquiry, *ibid.*, pp. 2-6.

84. *Ibid.*, pp. 112-14.

85. *Ibid.*, p. 131.

86. *Ibid.*, pp. 134-35.

87. *Ibid.*, pp. 125-26.

88. (1965-66) 8 *Crim. L.Q.* 408 at p. 423.

89. *Ibid.*, pp. 423-24.

90. *Ibid.*, pp. 425-26.

91. Government Reorganisation Act, S.O. 1972, c.1, s.97.

92. Interim Report of the Committee on Government Productivity No. 3, p. 24.

93. *Loc. cit.*

94. Statutes of Quebec, 1965, c.16.

95. Statutes of Quebec, 1886, c.99.

96. *Ibid.*, 1887, c.7, and repeated in R.S.Q. 1888, Title IV, c.3.

97. S.Q. 1964, c.9.

98. *La Police et la Sécurité des Citoyens*, issued on July 30, 1971.

99. *Ibid.*, pp. 125-126.

100. *Loc. cit.*

101. *Ibid.*, pp. 126-27.

102. See *Law Officers of the Crown*, Chap. 9.

103. See *post*, p. 39, n. 115.

104. *Op cit.*, p. 175.

105. See Edwards, *op. cit.*, Chap. 5.

106. C.O. 45, Vol. 157, *Journals of Legislative Assembly of Upper Canada*, March 8, 1829, Appendix, First Report of Committee on Finance. This was followed in 1831-32 by a series of resolutions passed by the Committee of Supply respecting the payment of salaries to the Law Officers of the Crown.

107. C.O. 42, Vol. 429,; G. series, Vol. 70, No. 118, March 6, 1833, Goderich to Lt. Governor Colborne.

108. G. series, Vol. 83, No. 242, November 8, 1837, letter from Colonial Secretary Glenelg to Lt. Governor Head.

109. See footnote 107 above. The full correspondence between the Colonial Office and the Government of the Province of Canada respecting this matter is also to be found in the *Journal of the Legislative Assembly of Upper Canada*, 1836, Appendix No. 28.

110. State Book F., Records of Executive Council, November 16, 1846. The same subject had occupied the minds of the Executive Council two years earlier, see State Book C, September 27, 1844.

111. *Loc. cit.*

112. See pp. 83-4, 272-3.

113. C.O. 45, Vol. 243. Appendix BB to First Report of the Select Committee which, regrettably, is unnumbered. For easy reference, see Edwards, *op. cit.*, pp. 166-67.

114. *Ibid.*, Q.40.

115. A random check of one year in each decade since Confederation reveals that there has been a considerable number of occasions when the Premier of a province has, at the same time, occupied the position of Attorney General. The following is representative of the years examined in the *Parliamentary Guide:*

Ontario	Oliver Mowat	A.G. &	Premier	1874
Quebec	H. Mercier	"	"	1887
Quebec	Homer Gouin	"	"	1910
Quebec	L.A. Taschereau	"	"	1922
Manitoba	W.J. Bracken	"	"	1935
Quebec	M. Duplessis	"	"	1948
Alberta	E.C. Manning	"	"	1956
New Brunswick	Louis J. Robichaud	"	"	1963
P.E.I.	Alex B. Campbell	"	"	1977

It is also worth noting that in the 1930's, Alberta's Attorney General, William Aberhart, who was not a lawyer and had never received any training in the law, was also Premier of the province and Minister of Education — see (1939) 17 *Can. B.R.* 416.

116. *Loc. cit.*

117. *Loc. cit.*

118. See Edwards *op. cit.*, pp. 167-68, and also the debates in the Canadian House of Commons on the Receiver General and Attorney General Bill 1878, especially the speech by the Prime Minister, Alexander Mackenzie, H.C. Debates, Vol. II, pp. 1591-92.

119. Edwards, *op. cit.*, pp. 168-69.

120. *Crown Law Practice in New Zealand* (1961) pp. 13, 21.

121. H.C. Debates, Vol. V, p. 5430, May 24, 1966.

122. H.C. Debates, Vol. V, p. 5524, May 25, 1966.

123. Edwards, *op. cit.*, Chap. 11.

124. *The Home Office* (1925) pp. 76-77.

125. *Loc. cit.*

126. See *Law Officers of the Crown*, pp. 185-198.

127. 42 & 43 Vict. c.22, and see Edwards, *op. cit.*, pp. 197, 361-66.

128. Reg. 1(c).

129. Edwards, *op. cit.*, pp. 197-98.

130. *Op. cit.*, pp. 185-198.

131. *Op. cit.*, p. 389.

132. *Op. cit.*, p. 389, n.85.

133. S.R. & O. 1946, No. 1467, L. 17, reg. 5. There was much speculation, following the setting up in the United Kingdom of the Royal Commission on Criminal Procedure that the 1946 Regulations would be subject to substantial changes in the near future. Indeed, in the announcement issued from 10 Downing Street on June 23, 1977, setting up the Royal Commission, it was stated: "The Government does not... intend the establishment of the Royal Commission, which will be concerned essentially with matters or principle, to hold up the improvements we are making within the existing framework. As part of this process... the Home Secretary and the Attorney General will be reviewing, as a matter of urgent study, the arrangements for prosecutions and interrelationship between the Director of Public Prosecutions and other prosecutors. This review will include the amendment of the Prosecution of Offences Regulations, 1946...". True in part to its forecast, the Government has replaced the 1946 regulations with a new statutory instrument, The Prosecution of Offences Regulations, 1978 (No. 1357 (L.33)) that took effect on January 1, 1979. Regulation 5 of the 1946 "charter", which I quote in the text (at p. 44), has not been repeated in the 1978 Regulations. Instead, reliance is placed on section 2 of the Prosecution of Offences Act, 1879, which states that the D.P.P. acts under the general superintendence of the Attorney General. Whether the two forms of language are truly synonymous may yet have to be determined.

134. Quoted in Edwards, *op. cit.*, pp. 222-23.

135. *Loc. cit.*

136. H.C. Debates, Vol. 483, col. 682, January 29, 1951.

137. *Op. cit.*, cols. 683-84.

138. Quoted in Edwards, *op. cit.*, p. 177.

138A. See P.R. Glazebrook (Ed.) *Reshaping the Criminal Law* 1978, pp. 364-390 (reprinted in (1979) 5 *Commonwealth Law Bulletin*, pp. 879-910).

139. This theme is developed more fully in *The Law Officers of the Crown*, pp. 252-256, the essence of which is that "any practice savouring of political pressure, either by the Executive or Parliament, being brought to bear upon the Law Officers when engaged in reaching a decision in any particular case is unconstitutional and is to be avoided at all costs. Acceptance of this first principle, however, in no way minimises the complementary doctrine of the Law Officers' ultimate responsibility to Parliament, in effect the House of Commons, for the exercise of their discretionary powers. To be explicit, it is conceived that after the termination of the particular criminal proceedings, that the Attorney General or the Solicitor General, as the case may be, is subject to questioning by members of the House in the same way as any other Minister of the Crown. Like any other Minister they are answerable for their ministerial actions" *op. cit.*, p. 224.

140. A verbatim copy of a typical pardon issued under the Royal Sign-Manual and countersigned by the Secretary of State for Home Affairs appears as the frontispiece to C.H. Rolph's *The Queen's Pardon*, 1978.

141. Provided to the author through the courtesy of the Home Office.

142. Home Office Memorandum 33391, quoted in Rolph, *op. cit.*, pp. 28-9.

143. See Frank Newsam, *The Home Office*, (New Whitehall Series), (1954) pp. 24, 26, 114-116, 119-121; O.R. Marshall "The Prerogative of Mercy" (1948) *Current Legal Problems*, pp. 104-125, and G. Marshall "Parliament and the Prerogative of Mercy" (1961) *Public Law*, pp. 8-25.

144. See Fenton Bresler, *Reprieve*, (1965), pp. 28-38.

145. Gone forever, it would seem, are the days when a pardon was effectuated under the instrumentality of the Great Seal. The initial reform, permitting a free or unconditional pardon for a

felon to be executed by warrant under the Royal Sign-Manual, countersigned by one of the Secretaries of State, was enacted by the Criminal Law Act, 1827 (7 & 8 Geo. 4. c. 28), s.13. The Criminal Law Act, 1967 (c.58), s.9, extended the procedure to all offences, declaring such pardons to be of like effect as a pardon issued under the Great Seal.

146. Bresler, *op. cit.*, pp. 36, 42-44.

147. Bresler, *op. cit.*, pp. 39-44.

148. Bresler, *op. cit.*, pp. 48-51.

149. 1 Vict., c.77.

150. See Bresler, *op. cit.*, pp. 52-53.

151. Bill No. 58; see *H.L. Debates*, Vol. 174, p. 1483, and Vol. 175, p. 252.

152. *H.C. Paper* 10438 (1866), pp. 198-209. This view was strongly supported by Mr. Walpole, a former Home Secretary, *ibid.*, pp. 69-70.

153. See J.A. Spender and C. Asquith, *Life of Lord Oxford and Asquith* (1932), Vol. II, p. 214, Roy Jenkins, *Asquith*, pp. 403-4, and D. Gwynn, *The Life and Death of Roger Casement* (1930), pp. 419-423. In his monograph on the *British Cabinet* (3rd ed. 1977), at p. 414, J.P. Mackintosh suggests that "when the death sentence was passed on young Cypriots for offences during the struggle for independence in the late 1950s the Cabinet might well have broken through the convention to consider the effect of executions upon world opinion or on negotiations about the future of the island". No documentary evidence has surfaced to confirm this hypothesis.

154. E.g., see R.I.M. Burnett, *Executive Discretion and Criminal Justice: The Prerogative of Mercy: New Zealand 1840-1853*, (1977), pp. 1-44. For the early Australian record see Todd, *Parliamentary Government in the British Colonies* (1st ed. 1880) pp. 251-267.

155. Patent Roll 26 Geo. III, Part V, No. 8.

156. Patent Roll 2 Vict. Part 19, No. 1. The confining of the exceptional circumstances to cases of murder only that appears in the Instructions issued to the Governor of Newfoundland in 1802 and 1804 is consistent with the denial of jurisdiction in cases of treason to the criminal courts in that colony contained in the same instructions. See Patent Roll 42 Geo. III, Part VI, Nos. 8 and 15.

157. *Public Archives of Canada Report*, 1906, p. 118.

158. *Loc. cit.* This requirement, recalling as it does the English practice in the eighteenth century of the Recorder of London attending in person meetings of the Privy Council to consider death sentences imposed by judges at the Old Bailey (see *ante*, footnote 146), was discontinued in the Royal Instructions issued to Governor Monck in 1867 (see *Public Archives of Canada Report* 1906, p. 135). Interestingly, so I am informed, until the recent abolition of capital punishment in Australia, this practice was continued in the State of Victoria where the presiding judge in a murder trial was invited to attend the meeting of the Executive Council at which the question of exercising the prerogative of mercy was discussed, prior to making a recommendation to the Governor of the State.

159. *Public Archives of Canada Report*, 1906, p. 128.

160. *Public Archives of Canada Report*, 1906, p. 135.

161. Quoted in Todd *op. cit.*, pp. 272-3. For the interesting story of the debate between the Canadian Minister of Justice (Mr. Blake) and the Colonial Secretary (Lord Carnarvon) which preceded the issuance of the 1878 Royal Instructions see Todd *op. cit.*, pp. 269-271, and *Canada Sess. Papers*, 1879, no. 181.

162. 81 *The Canada Gazette*, Part 1, pp. 3015-6 (October 11, 1947), which terms are repeated verbatim in the latest instructions to the present Governor General. The full text is also set forth in the *Revised Statutes of Canada*, 1970, Appx. 35. The same clause is to be found in the Instructions to the Governor General of Australia (*Parliamentary Papers*, 1901-2, Vol. 2, p. 831) which has continued unchanged to the present day. Given the constitutional arrangements in Australia, where criminal law falls primarily within the jurisdiction of the respective States it is surprising to note the absence of any comparable provision in the Letters Patent to the Governor of Victoria, New South Wales, Queensland etc. — see *Commonwealth Statutory Rules*, 1901-1956, Vol. 5, pp.

5326-5342 and R.D. Lumb, *The Constitutions of the Australian States*, 4th ed., App. IV and V. Nevertheless, we may confidently assume that no Governor would elect to act in matters of pardon other than in accordance with the advice of the State Executive Council.

163.   The provisions of the present Code, s.683, replicate the terms of section 966 in the first Criminal Code of 1892 which, in turn, was adapted from the Punishments, Pardons, etc. Act, 1886 (Can.), (49 Vict. c. 181) ss. 38 and 39, and its predecessor, the Criminal Procedure Act, 1869 (Can.) (32 & 33 Vict. c. 29), ss. 125, 126. Significantly, all the legislation prior to 1953-54 referred to "The Crown" as extending the royal mercy or granting a pardon. In the revised Criminal Code, 1953-54, s. 655 we find, for the first time, reference to "The Governor in Council" as the constitutional authority for granting a free or conditional pardon.

164.   See Criminal Code, 1953-54, section 656 of which reads as follows:

"656.   (1) The Governor in Council may commute a sentence of death to imprisonment in the penitentiary for life, or for any term of years not less than two years, or to imprisonment in a prison other than a penitentiary for a period of less than two years.

(2) A copy of an instrument duly certified by the Clerk of the Privy Council or a writing under the hand of the Minister of Justice or Deputy Minister of Justice declaring that a sentence of death is commuted is sufficient notice to and authority for all persons having control over the prisoner to do all things necessary to give effect to the commutation."

Capital punishment was abolished in Canada by the Criminal Law Amendment Act (No. 2) 1976, c. 105. In its place convictions for first or second degree murder carry a mandatory sentence of life imprisonment (Code, s. 218), the consequences of which differ only in terms of eligibility for parole (Code, ss. 669-674). During the five year trial period that preceded the ultimate total abolition of the death penalty, release was contingent on the final approval of the Governor in Council based on the recommendation of the Solicitor General of Canada (Code, s. 684).

165.   Earlier in this study, (*ante* pp. 22-23), an account was given of the interplay within the Department of Justice in the allocation of administrative responsibilities between the Minister of Justice and the Solicitor General, with respect to both the review of a petitioner's file for clemency in a capital case and the formal recommendation to the Executive Council. Where reference is made to the Minister of Justice (or the Deputy Minister) the old Code, (R.S.C. 1927, c. 36, s. 1077) speaks of the notice of commutation being signed by the Secretary of State of Canada (or the Under Secretary of State), as to which office see *ante* p. 9. See too footnote 163 *supra* for the later statutory changes in ministerial responsibility for pardons.

166.   It reads "The President ... shall have power to grant reprieves and pardons for offences against the United States except in cases of impeachment". The exception is derived from, and parallels that contained in, the English Act of Settlement, 1700 (12 & 13 Will. III, c.2, s.3), which provides that "no pardon under the Great Seal of England be pleadable to an impeachment by the Commons in Parliament".

167.   The period of activity with respect to which immunity from prosecution was conferred is stated in the presidential pardon as extending from January 20, 1969 through August 9, 1974. (i.e. Nixon's first term as President of the United States plus that portion of his second term in office which terminated with his resignation.

168.   *Reported in U.S. News and World Report*, October 28, 1974. Mr. Ford's two-hour testimony before the Committee was an historic occasion, representing, as it did, the first recorded appearance of a United States President before a Congressional Committee to submit to personal interrogation. It is of interest to note that in the course of the debates at the Federal Convention which led to the adoption of the United States Constitution a motion to insert "after conviction" in the language which became Article II, section 2 was withdrawn after it had been pointed out that pre-conviction pardons "might be necessary to obtain the testimony of accomplices"; M. Farrand, *The Records of the Federal Convention of 1787* (1937), Vol. 2, p. 426, quoted in H.C. Macgill's article (see next footnote). The same article quotes the opinion of Attorney General William Witt in 1820 that the Constitution permitted pre-conviction pardons, though the general practice of granting pardons only following conviction or confession represented the sounder policy, *Opinions of the Attorney General* (1852), Vol. 1, pp. 343-44. Among the individual states, it appears that the constitutions of 32 states expressly confine the Governor's powers to post-conviction relief, whereas 6 states follow the model of the federal constitution — Macgill, *op. cit.*, pp. 68-69.

169. For a thorough analysis of the United States authorities on the several aspects of this question, see H.C. Macgill: "The Nixon Pardon: Limits on the Benign Prerogative" (1974-75) 7 *Connecticut L.R.*, 56-92.

170. Among the early writers, whose exposition of the common law is generally relied upon as authoritative, the following may be cited:

Coke, *Third Institute*, (1644), cap. CV, p. 233:

"A pardon is a work of mercy, whereby the King either before attainder, sentence, or conviction, or after forgiveth any crime, offence, punishment, execution, right, title, debt or duty, Temporal or Ecclesiastical ..."

Blackstone, *Commentaries* (1765) Book IV, pp. 394-5:

"The King's charter of pardon must be specially pleaded, and that at a proper time .... But if a man avails himself thereof as soon as by courts of law he may, a pardon may either be pleaded upon arraignment, or in arrest of judgment, or in the present stage of proceedings, in bar of execution".

See too, Hawkins, *Pleas of the Crown*, Vol. II, (1721), sections 33 and 54.

171. Cf. *post*, footnote 176.

172. The same language is to be found in the Code of 1892, s.970, and in the Pardon and Commutation of Sentences Act, 1886, s.42.

173. See, e.g. the English Criminal Law Act 1967 (c.58), s.9, Cf. the Canadian Criminal Records Act, R.S.C. 1970, First Supp. c.12, s.9 of which states: "Nothing in this Act in any manner limits or affects the provisions of the Criminal Code, or the Letters Patent Constituting the Office of Governor General of Canada, relating to pardons ..." The 1970 Act provides for a procedure whereby those who have been convicted of offences and have subsequently rehabilitated themselves can apply for a pardon that, if granted by the Governor in Council, vacates the conviction(s) and removes any consequential disqualifications. Recommendations regarding the issuance of a pardon are made to the Governor in Council by the National Parole Board, through the office of the Solicitor General, after satisfying itself as to the good conduct of the offender.

174. Quoted in Todd *op. cit.*, p. 272, and *Canada Sess. Papers*, 1879, No. 14.

175. See *ante* footnote 162.

176. Todd, *loc. cit.*

177. Home Office historical note on the subject of "Pardons before conviction", kindly forwarded to this author. The same document states: "When in 1947 counsel prosecuting in a criminal case inquired as to the possibility of using the prerogative in that way he was informed, after consultation with the Director of Public Prosecutions, that it was no longer the practice to grant free pardons for this purpose".

178. In an application to the Divisional Court for judicial review of the D.P.P.'s decision, Thorpe unsuccessfully challenged the immunity granted to one of the chief Crown witnesses — see *The Times*, November 16, 1978. See, too, the statement by the Attorney General in the House of Commons on the same subject, *The Times*, November 28, 1978. For a further and unprecedented challenge to the D.P.P.'s exercise of his statutory powers in granting immunity to one of the participants in a crime see the recent judgment of Jones, J., in *Turner* v. *D.P.P.* (1979) 68 Cr. App. Rep. 70.

179. See, e.g., Wade and Phillips, *Constitutional and Administrative Law* (9th ed. by A.W. Bradley) p. 338, and S.A. de Smith, *Constitutional and Administrative Law* (1971), p. 128, who writes: "It would seem that a pardon may be granted *before* conviction; but this power is never exercised. The line between pardon before conviction and the unlawful exercise of dispensing power is thin". R.F.V. Heuston, on the other hand, in his *Essays in Constitutional Law* (2nd ed.), makes no reference to modern English practice and states without qualification, "... the monarch may pardon any offence against the criminal law whether before or after conviction" (p. 69). A review of the "independence" constitutions within the Commonwealth, negotiated with the U.K. Government prior to the transfer of sovereignty, provides substantial support for a pre-conviction limitation on the pardoning power. Examples are to be found in the constitutions of Kenya (1963), Guyana (1966), Barbados (1966), the Bahamas (1973), Zambia (1973) and St. Lucia (1978). In comparison, reference may be had to Trinidad and Tobago which, at the time of acquiring its

independence in 1962, followed the pattern described above. Subsequently, in 1976, the power of its President was enlarged to permit the granting of a pardon before or after conviction. The Nigeria Constitution (1963) and that of Malawi (1966) contain earlier precedents of the more extensive availability of the presidential pardoning power.

179A. It is noteworthy that in a circular dispatch addressed by the Colonial Secretary to all the colonial governors on November 1, 1871 it was stated that in England a pardon is not granted before the trial of an offender. At the same time it was recognised that a proclamation of amnesty for past offences against the Crown is within the Royal Prerogative, examples of which include those issued by Lord Durham, Governor General of Canada in 1838; Sir George Grey, Governor of New Zealand in 1865; and by Lord Dufferin, Governor General of Canada in 1875 — see Todd, *op. cit.*, pp. 267-68.

180. Cap. 76, s.2.

181. S.I. 1979, No. 820, s.2.

182. See Geoffrey Marshall's essay on "Parliament and the Prerogative of Mercy" [1961] *Public Law*, pp. 8-25, and cf. the position taken by O.R. Marshall in "The Prerogative of Mercy" [1948] *Current Legal Problems* 104 at pp. 106, 113, 117.

183. The precedents and arguments concerning this subject are analysed in Edwards, *The Law Officers of the Crown* pp. 224-25 and p. 253 *et seq.*

184. Wade & Phillips, *op. cit.*, p. 11.

185. Cmnd. 1728. For the background to the setting up of the 1962 Royal Commission see T.A. Critchley: *A History of Police in England & Wales* (Revised edition 1978), pp. 270-275.

186. Cmnd. 1222, paras. 32-34.

187. Cmnd. 1728, paras. 61-78. The leading authorities are *Fisher v. Oldham Corporation* [1930] 2 K.B. 364 and *Attorney General for N.S.W. v. Perpetual Trustee Co.* [1955] A.C. 477.

188. Cmnd. 1728, para. 68.

189. *Ibid.*, para. 87. The position in Scotland, it was recognised, is somewhat different from that which prevails in England and Wales. Under the Police (Scotland) Act, 1956, s.4(3), chief constables are required to comply with such lawful instructions as they may receive from the procurator fiscal (the public prosecutor) in relation to the investigation of offences. It is an open question as to where exactly the provincial Crown prosecutor in Canada falls within this kind of relationship with the police.

190. *Ibid.*, para. 89.

191. *Loc. cit.* and see also paras. 91-99.

192. *Ibid.*, para. 91.

193. 330 H.C. Debates, 3s. c.1174.

194. *Loc. cit.*

195. *Ibid.*, para. 98.

196. *Loc. cit.*

197. *Ibid.*, para. 94.

198. *Ibid.*, paras. 100-111.

199. *Ibid.*, para. 114.

200. The Law Society, it is worth noting, in its brief to the Royal Commission recommended that the control of police forces should be vested in chief constables who, in turn, would be placed under the general direction of a police commission. The commission would be accountable to Parliament through the Home Secretary. This idea, so familiar to us in Canada, was not adopted by the Royal Commission on the Police.

201. *Ibid.*, para. 230.

202. *Ibid.*, para. 231.

203. For a helpful review of this important piece of legislation see D.W. Pollard's article in [1966] *Public Law*, 35-64, also T.A. Critchley: *A History of Police in England and Wales*, pp. 293-295.

204. The fullest treatment of the Home Secretary's answerability to Parliament prior to the Police Act, 1964, is to be found in Critchley, *loc. cit.*, p. 270 *et seq.*

205. These inter-connecting links are developed more fully in the research paper on the United Kingdom, prepared by Professor D.G.T. Williams for the present Commission.

206. A little light on the autonomous character of the Special Branches is cast by Sir Robert Mark, former Commissioner of the Metropolitan London Police, in his stimulating autobiography entitled *In the Office of Constable*, 1978, at p. 296. Confirmation of the existence of special branches in other police forces outside London was given by the Parliamentary Under Secretary of State for the Home Department in 1977. Speaking in the House of Commons, Dr. Shirley Summerskill stated: "There is no national Special Branch. There could, therefore, be no annual report of the Special Branch. Only in the annual reports of each chief constable can there be annual reports of individual branches. Although it coordinates the collection of intelligence affecting the activities of the Irish Republican Army, Metropolitan [London] Police Special Branch in no sense controls the Special Branches of other forces": *H.C. Debates*, Vol. 931, Col. 810, May 5, 1977.

207. *Lord Denning's Report*, the simple but graphic title given to the ensuing report, was presented to Parliament by the Prime Minister in September 1963, a mere 3 months from the date of the original commission — see Cmnd. 2152.

208. *Ibid.*, para. 1.

209. *Ibid.*, para. 270.

210. *Ibid.*, para. 283.

211. *Ibid.*, paras. 284-286.

212. *Ibid.*, para. 273.

213. Attention to this fact was drawn in the *Report of the [Mackenzie] Royal Commission on Security* (1969) pp. 14-15, Such legislative authority as does exist is derived from section 44(e) of the R.C.M.P. Act, S.C. 1959, c.54 — which provides that "in addition to the duties prescribed by the Act, it is the duty of the force... (e) to maintain and operate such security and intelligence services as may be required by the Minister". Reference must also be made to the Commissioner's Standing Orders for which provision is made in section 21(2) of the 1959 Act.

214. *Loc. cit.*

215. *Loc. cit.*

216. *Ibid.*, para. 277.

217. *Ibid*, para. 230.

218. *Ibid.*, para. 236.

219. *Ibid.*, para. 237.

220. *Ibid.*, para. 238.

221. This conclusion is emphasized by Lord Denning in paragraph 239(1) of his Report. He states that the majority view amongst the witnesses that he had examined was that "in all cases there should be a clear and unambiguous channel to the Home Secretary" and that the great body of opinion before him was that national security should be dealt with as the responsibility of the Home Secretary and not as the responsibility of a separate Minister [of National Security], *ibid.*, paras. 240-42.

222. Support for this exposition of the respective roles of the Prime Minister and the Home Secretary is to be found in the recent statement made by the Parliamentary Under Secretary of State for the Home Department in the House of Commons during a debate concerning the British Security Service. "Members" it was said "are entirely justified in seeking to be assured that Ministers are satisfied of the competence, integrity and loyalty of the Service. That, more than the accuracy or otherwise of allegations of what happened or did not happen on particular occasions

in the past, is the serious point in all this. The House is entitled to look to the Ministers to whom the security service is answerable and accountable — that is, the Home Secretary and in the last resort the Prime Minister — to accept responsibility that all is well in this respect. As to that, the tradition in this country is that the service is accountable to Ministers. Parliament accepts that the accountability must be to Ministers rather than to Parliament, and trusts Ministers to discharge that responsibility faithfully": *H.C. Debates*, vol. 936, col. 1224, July 28, 1977.

223. See *post*, p. 92, footnote 303.

224. See H.C. Debates, Vol. 121, pp. 593-4, Nov. 3, 1977. An earlier illustration is the Cabinet directive of 1971 as to the extent to which surveillance of university campuses would be allowed. Reference to these guidelines was made by Mr. Francis Fox, when Solicitor General, before the House of Commons Standing Committee on Justice and Legal Affairs, November 29, 1977, p. 3:17. In effect, these guidelines reiterated the principles announced in 1963 by Prime Minister Pearson to the Canadian Association of University Teachers, that there would be no surveillance of university campuses as such but individuals would not be immune from surveillance just because they happened to be working in a university. Cf. footnote 305, *post*. The substance of Cabinet Directive No. 35 of 1963, dealing with security in the public service of Canada, was communicated to the House of Commons by Mr. Pearson on October 25, 1963 — H.C. Debates, Vol. 4, pp. 4043-5 and also *ibid.*, Vol. 5, pp. 5497, 5499, July 11, 1973.

225. See *ante*, p. 61.

226. See *ante*, pp. 56-7.

227. See Edwards, *Law Officers of the Crown*, pp. 224-25, 231, 243-46, 253-56, 260-61.

228. H.C. Debates, Vol. 121, pp. 3881-83, March 17, 1978.

229. In the event, the Attorney General's fiat, required under section 12 of the Official Secrets Act, was granted with respect to the prosecution of the Toronto Sun Publishing Ltd., together with its publisher and editor, but declined in the case of Mr. Tom Cossitt, M.P. No explanatory reasons by the Attorney General of Canada were forthcoming in the only other recent prosecution under the Official Secrets Act, *R* v. *Treu* (1978). The accused in that case was charged with "unlawfully retaining" (s.4(1)(a)) and "failing to take reasonable care of" (s.4(1)(d)) N.A.T.O. documents relating to secret air communication systems that he had obtained as an employee of the Northern Electric Company which was party to a defence contract with N.A.T.O. Treu's conviction was reversed on appeal to the Quebec Court of Appeal — see Globe & Mail, Feb. 21, 1979.

230. The Toronto newspaper, together with its publisher and editor, were charged under the Official Secrets Act, s.4(1)(a) and s.4(3), after printing an article based on a R.C.M.P. report entitled "Canadian related activities of the Russian Intelligence Services". Parts of the same document had previously been made public, independently of the *Sun* article, in a CTV television broadcast and during exchanges in the House of Commons. On April 23, 1979 the preliminary hearing concluded with the discharge of the accused, there being insufficient evidence, in the opinion of the Provincial Court Judge, to place the accused on trial. The previous publicity accorded to the report, classified "Top Secret — For Canadian eyes only", in the view of the court, had brought the "shopworn" document into the public domain and thus outside the purview of the Official Secrets Act.

231. *Loc. cit.*

232. *Loc. cit.*

233. H.C. Debates, Vol. II, p. 1147, May 11, 1965.

234. *Ibid.*, p. 1148. Earlier, in his prepared statement to the House of Commons on the involvement of Canadians in Russian espionage acts, the Prime Minister had stated, "Certainly there can be no question of prosecution for wrongdoing in this case; quite the contrary", *ibid.*, p. 1139. The Minister of Justice, Mr. Favreau, contributed nothing to the debate.

235. H.C. Debates, Vol. III, pp. 2997-98, June 29, 1965.

236. H.C. Debates, Vol. VII, pp. 7684-7691, September 4, 1964.

237. *Ibid.*, p. 7690.

238. H.C. Debates, Vol. VI, pp. 6083, 6085, July 28, 1964.

239. As reported in the *Toronto Star*, May 5, 1979 and the *Ottawa Journal* of the same date.

240. See *R. v. Knechtel* (1975) 23 C.C.C. 545 and *R. v. Pelletier* (1974) 18 C.C.C. (2d) 516 at pp. 521-22.

241. See *ante*, pp. 104-5.

242. For a remarkable instance of a legislative body being invited by the Government of the day to determine whether criminal proceedings should be instituted, see the Dutch Parliament's handling of the Prince Bernhard affair in 1976 — *The Times*, August 27, 28 and 31, 1976.

243. No doubt Mr. Basford had in mind the findings of the Select Committee of the British House of Commons on the *Duncan Sandys case* in 1939, see H.C. Paper 101.

244. H.C. Debates, Vol. 121, pp. 3881-3883, March 17, 1978. See also footnote 230.

245. *Loc. cit.*

246. See, for example, Mr. Favreau's use of the phrase when announcing the setting up of the Dorion Inquiry, H.C. Debates, Vol. X, p. 10427, November 24, 1964, — "I have to assert now that I have had advice from the law officers of the crown". Prime Minister Trudeau used the phrase in the same context when referring to possible limitations on the testimony that Ministers might give before the McDonald Commission in Inquiry: "If there were a subpoena... issued to any member of this government, he would be guided by the law officers of the crown as to what he would be entitled to say or not say under the Official Secrets Act" — H.C. Debates, Vol. 121, p. 684, November 8, 1977. Other instances will be found in H.C. Debates, Vol. II, p. 1682, February 23, 1966. "The law officers of the Crown had advised against instituting criminal proceedings... and proceedings were not taken" *per* Lucien Cardin, Minister of Justice; and Mr. Diefenbaker"... what legal matters come to the attention of the Minister of Justice? He is not in the position of having such things come to his attention because the law officers of the Crown look after these various things" — H.C. Debates, Vol. V, p. 4878, May 9, 1966.

247. See *ante*, footnote 1, and Appendix A to this study.

248. Statutes of Ontario, 1962-63, c.106, s.4 and see R.S.O. 1970, c.351, ss.40-41.

249. Statutes of Quebec, 1968, c.17, s.8.

250. Statutes of Alberta, 1971, c.85, s.5.

251. Statutes of Manitoba, 1971, c.85, s.22(1).

252. Statutes of Nova Scotia, 1974, c.9, s.4.

253. Statutes of Saskatchewan, 1973-4, c.77, s.7.

254. Statutes of British Columbia, 1974, c.64, s.2.

255. Statutes of New Brunswick, 1977, c.P-9.2, s.18. This statute is noteworthy for its adoption of a questionable defence to offences created by the provincial legislature, the repercussions to which defence have yet to manifest themselves. According to section 3(4) of the New Brunswick Police Act:

"A member of the Royal Canadian Mounted Police or a member of a police force shall not be convicted of a violation of any Provincial statute if it is made to appear to the judge before whom the complaint is heard that the person charged with the offence committed the offence for the purpose of obtaining evidence or in carrying out his lawful duties."

The above provision is patterned on the corresponding section 13 in the Prince Edward Island Police Act (R.S.P.E.I., 1974, c.P-9) which defines the defence as extending to violations "while acting under instructions given by the Minister of Justice or the officer commanding [the police force] ... for the purpose of obtaining evidence". The P.E.I. law was first introduced in 1930 (Laws of P.E.I., c.16, s.14). The earliest precedent for this kind of statutory exemption in Canadian law that I have been able to discover was enacted in New Brunswick in 1927 (*Laws*, c.9, s.3) which stated: "No action shall be brought against the ... chief of police or any ... policemen for anything done by them in the apparent discharge of their duty, unless with the consent of the Attorney General".

256. Ontario Legislature Debates, 1961-62, Vol. 1, p. 284, December 11, 1961.

257. For a rare insight into the problems that can arise in defining this kind of relationship within the province of New Brunswick see the *Report of the [Hughes] Commission of Inquiry into matters relating to the Department of Justice and the R.C.M.P., 1978*, and also a paper delivered to the New Brunswick Bar Association by Gordon F. Gregory, Deputy Minister of Justice of the province, entitled "Police Power and the role of the Minister of Justice" which has since been published in (1979) 27 *Chitty's L.J.* 13-18.

258. This relationship is developed in the annual report of the Quebec Police Commission 1973, p. 18. The precise legalities of the arrangements deserves closer study. Since writing this study, the question has come before the Alberta Supreme Court in *Re Putnam and Cramer, per* Miller, J., whose unreported judgment was delivered on August 3, 1979 (Docket No. 7903-00570). An appeal from the trial judge's decision is pending before the Alberta Court of Appeal.

259. Ontario Police Act, R.S.O. 1970, c.351, s.41(1).

260. *Loc. cit.* Similar provisions are to be found in the Police Acts of the other provinces which have set up Police Commissions.

261. *Op. cit.*, s.6(2).

262. *Op. cit.*, s.56.

263. Under the terms of a Government Bill introduced in the Ontario Legislature on June 18, 1979 the requirement, under the Ontario Police Act, that one member of some Boards of police commissioners must be a County or District Court judge would be removed. The proposed change would not alter the composition of the Metropolitan Toronto Board of Police Commissioners which is governed by the Municipality of Metropolitan Toronto Act, R.S.O. 1970, 295, s.177(1).

264. Dicey, A.V., *Introduction to the Study of the Law of the Constitution*, 9th edition, London, Macmillan, 1959, pp. 325-327.

265. For the United Kingdom position, see B. Schwartz and H.W.R. Wade, *Legal Control of Government* (1972), Ch. 8, and Crown Proceedings Act, 1949. Each of the Canadian provinces has legislation that parallel the Ontario Proceedings against the Crown Act, R.S.O. 1970, c.365. Federally, see Crown Liability Act 1952-53, c.30, R.S.C. 1970, c.C.38.

266. *Constitutional and Administrative Law*, 1971, p. 174.

267. *Per* Lord Home, *The Observer*, September 16, 1962. In the same article the former Prime Minister said: "...no Minister can make a really important move without consulting the Prime Minister, and if the Prime Minister wanted to take a certain step the Cabinet Minister concerned would either have to agree, argue it out in Cabinet, or resign". Compare P. Gordon Walker's opinion: "A strong Prime Minister can be very strong. He can sometimes commit the Cabinet by acts or words. But he cannot *habitually* or often do so. A Prime Minister who habitually ignored the Cabinet or behaved as if Prime Ministerial government were a reality — such a Prime Minister could rapidly come to grief... The Prime Minister can exercise his greatly enhanced powers if he carries his cabinet with him" — *The Cabinet* (1970) p. 95, (the author's italics).

268. See *de Smith, op. cit.*, p. 173.

269. H.C. Debates, Vol. 121, p. 2350, January 30, 1978.

270. This event is fully covered in *Lord Denning's Report*, Cmnd. 2152 (1963), *ante*, pp. 58-9.

271. See *Law Officers of the Crown*, p. 261.

272. See G. Wilson: *Cases and Materials on Constitutional and Administrative Law* (2nd ed.), 1976, pp. 138, 144.

273. In addition to the House of Commons debates on this event reference should be made to Prime Minister Pearson's account of the circumstances surrounding Mr. Favreau's resignation — see *Mike (the Memoirs of Lester B. Pearson)*, Vol. 3, pp. 161-172.

274. See H.C. Debates, Vol. XI, p. 11823, March 16, 1976. As a result of the "judges' affair" Prime Minister Trudeau made public guidelines concerning future ministerial conduct in relation to the judiciary, the gist of which is to totally proscribe direct communications between ministers and members of the Bench concerning any matter which they have before them in their judicial capacities, except through the Minister of Justice, his duly authorized officials or counsel acting for him. (See H.C. Debates, Vol. XI, p. 11771, March 12, 1976.) Two years later, John

Munro, the Minister of Labour, violated the guidelines and paid the penalty of resignation from the Cabinet — see *Globe and Mail*, September 8 & 9, 1978. At the same time, in Ontario, following disclosure of the fact that the Solicitor General, George Kerr, had telephoned an Assistant Crown Attorney to intercede on behalf of a constituent, the provincial Premier's stance was less than wholly convincing. In acknowledging the wrongfulness of the Solicitor General's intervention Mr. Davis, first, excused it on the ground that it was well motivated and then, apparently in the wake of the Munro resignation, the Premier reversed his stand and Kerr was no longer a member of the Ontario Government — see *Globe and Mail*, September 9 and 11, 1978.

275. *Op. cit.*, pp. 11842-3, March 16, 1976.

276. de Smith, *op. cit.* p. 175. Earlier in the same work the author took a more sober view of the doctrine, reminding his readers that: "...no definition of collective responsibility is likely to give satisfaction because the outlines of the concept are vague and blurred. It can be described at a high level of generality; it can be illustrated by specific examples; a neat but comprehensive set of propositions cannot be devised, if only because the gulf between traditional constitutional theory (to which lip service may still be paid) and political practice."

277. See *post*, p. 90. For a strong defence of the doctrine of collective responsibility see the speech by Prime Minister Trudeau in H.C. Debates, Vol. VIII, pp. 6013-6015, May 22, 1975.

278. *Op. cit.*, p. 177.

279. *Op. cit.*, p. 179. See too, the succinct exposition of the same subject in the Glassco Report, 1962, Vol. 1, Chap. 3; Vol. 5, Chap. 2.

280. H.C. Debates, Vol. 552, Cols. 1751-60, May 14, 1956.

281. *Loc. cit.*

282. See Cmnd. 9176 (1953); Cmnd. 9220 (1954); D.N. Chester (1951) 32 *Public Administration* 389 and J.A.G. Griffith (1955) 18 *M.L.R.* 557. The minister's resignation, in these circumstances, has generally come to be regarded as exceptional, the contrast usually drawn is with the *Ferranti case* in 1964 in which the Ministry of Aviation was severely criticised by the Comptroller and Auditor General for its lack of direction and collaboration between the branches within the Ministry. The Minister, Mr. Julian Amery, did not tender his resignation and it was not sought by the Prime Minister. For the parliamentary debate, see July 30, 1964.

283. de Smith, *op. cit.*, p. 175.

284. 530 H.C. Debates, 5s., c.1285, July 20, 1954.

285. Professor de Smith formulates the applicable principle somewhat differently, saying: "In answering questions, or in replying to a debate, he cannot be expected to accept that he is himself culpable whenever a departmental official has committed a dishonest act or has disobeyed instructions. He is entitled to explain in public what has occurred; but he cannot totally absolve himself of responsibility. To use a colloquialism which, eluding exact definition, is still well understood, he must in the last resort, 'carry the can'. If maladministration within his Department is attributable to bad organisation or procedures or defective supervision, or exists on such a large scale or at so high a level that he ought to have been able to prevent it, then he is to some degree blameworthy" — *op. cit.*, p. 174.

286. H.C. Paper 393 of 1971-72, July 17, 1972, see Appendix 9. Amongst the list of matters about which successive Administrations have refused to answer questions in the Westminster Parliament are the following: details of investigations by the Director of Public Prosecutions, detailed expenditure within Universities, telephone tapping, security service operations, police operational matters, day to day matters pertaining to the nationalised industries.

287. 848 H.C. Debates, 5s., col. 1970, December 18, 1972. Lately, the Speaker of the British House of Commons has intervened to assist a backbencher M.P. who was thwarted in his attempts to discover the contents of the latest list of forbidden parliamentary questions — see *The Times*, April 24, 1978.

288. In his *Judicial Review of Administrative Action* (2nd ed.), Professor de Smith writes (pp. 181-184): "An authority entrusted with a discretion must not, in the purported exercise of its discretion, act under the dictation of another body .... All authorities entrusted with statutory discretions, whether they be executive officers or members of administration tribunals, must be guided by considerations of public policy, and in some contexts the policy of the existing Govern-

ment will be a relevant factor in weighing those considerations; but this will not absolve them from their duty to exercise their individual judgment." Professor H.W.R. Wade, in a review of the Commonwealth authorities on the subject, puts forward the same conclusions in his *Administrative Law* (4th ed.) pp. 315-317. As I see it, the same principles should obtain where it is the Minister himself who is charged with the exercise of an independent discretionary power and surrenders it to the dictates of his Cabinet colleagues.

289. In Australia, the High Court has recently handed down a landmark decision in *Sankey* v. *Whitlam et al.* (1978) 53 A.L.J.R. 11, which makes substantial inroads into the inviolability, for the purposes of invoking Crown privilege, of Government documents relating to matters of high policy, including records of Cabinet discussions and official minutes of advice to Ministers. In Canada also, two recent pronouncements, both concerning the McDonald Commission of Inquiry, on the subject of Crown privilege as it extends to Cabinet minutes and papers, should be noted. First, is the Statement issued by the Commission and reported in (1979) 44 C.C.C. (2d) 220-222, and secondly, the Order in Council, P.C. 1979-887, issued on March 22, 1979 defining the conditions under which the Commissioners should have access to the minutes of any Cabinet or Cabinet Committee meeting which relate to the terms of the Commission as set out in Order in Council, P.C. 1977-1911.

290. de Smith *op. cit.*, pp. 173-180, and Wade *op. cit.*, pp. 313-315.

291. See my article "Politics and the integrity of criminal prosecutions", referred to in footnote 138A, at pp. 376-377.

292. 30 and 31 Vict. c.3, see sections 9, 10 and 11. For the full text of the B.N.A. Act and its subsequent amendments see R.S.C. 1970, Appendix II.

293. 1977, Carswell, at p. 9.

294. (1946) 12 *Can. Jo. of Economics & Political Science*, pp. 261-281.

295. *Op. cit.*, pp. 268-69.

296. See especially H.C. Debates, Vol. 13, pp. 14030-1, June 1, 1976, for the statement by the Minister of Supply and Services (Mr. Goyer) in which he declared: "I take my ministerial responsibilities very seriously with regard to the policies and administrative practices of my Department. Accordingly, I will stand by my officials and I accept responsibility for errors of judgment, mistakes made in good faith and inadvertent errors. But I do not believe that ministerial responsibility extends to cases of misinformation or gross negligence... The public has a right to be accurately informed. My ministerial responsibility in this case is to see that these rights are preserved. Consequently Mr. L.H. Stopforth has been removed from his function as deputy head of the project office". The Minister repeated his accusation against the public servant outside the House of Commons and was sued for libel. Judgment by Lieff J. was given in favour of Mr. Stopforth, the damages being assessed at $10,000 plus costs — S.C.O. April 13, 1978.

297. H.C. Debates, Vol. 121, pp. 2566-7, February 6, 1978.

298. See, e.g., the Speaker's ruling reported in H.C. Debates, Vol. 120, p. 6851, June 20, 1977: "Can members ask a question of a minister in that minister's former capacity? The clear answer given time and time again, without any doubt about our practices and precedents, has been no. It is tied very directly to the theory of ministerial responsibility, that the present incumbent of a ministerial office has responsibility which goes back for all time (*sic*). It does not stop at the time that that incumbent took office. Therefore there cannot be two people responsible to the House in the parliamentary sense for that continuing responsibility".

299. H.C. Debates, Vol. 121, p. 2566, February 6, 1978.

300. *Op. cit.*, p. 2558.

301. H.C. Debates, Vol. 121, p. 564, November 2, 1977.

302. *Ibid.*, p. 567.

303. The process of reaching this decision before communicating it to the Security Service was explained by Warren Allmand, the then Solicitor General, in H.C. Debates, Vol. XIII, p. 13224, May 6, 1976, where he stated: "That cabinet decision was based on a document that I had submitted to Cabinet. It had first been screened or dealt with by the Cabinet Committee on Security [and] Intelligence. A decision had been made and submitted to full Cabinet. Cabinet confirmed it and it was passed on to the R.C.M.P. ... It was really a Cabinet decision. It dealt with general

operations only of the Security Service and did not deal with security screening of applicants for the public service." Although the essential elements of this mandate were revealed to the House of Commons by Solicitor General Francis Fox on October 28, 1977, see H.C. Debates, Vol. 121, p. 394, it was not until July 13, 1978 that the decision was made to declassify the document and release it for public scrutiny.

304. H.C. Debates, Vol. 121, pp. 593-4, November 3, 1977.

305. An article by Geoffrey Stevens in the *Globe and Mail* on April 26, 1978 revealed the existence of a document, purportedly derived from a R.C.M.P. manual, in which policy instructions were issued by the Security Service in 1971 to members of the federal police force concerning their responsibility to report on candidates of all political persuasions who were seeking political office in the federal, provincial and municipal spheres and who were considered of security interest. Confirmation of the existence of the documents referred to in the *Globe and Mail* article was reluctantly extracted by the Opposition from the Solicitor General, J.J. Blais — H.C. Debates, Vol. 121, pp. 4972-3, April 28, 1978. Blais, it should be noted, neither confirmed nor denied the accuracy of the entire newspaper story. In defence of the policy reflected in the R.C.M.P. directive the Solicitor General and the Prime Minister, first, distinguished between the position of *individuals* who were the subject of concern by the Security Service and that of *legitimate political parties* which the Security Service had been expressly instructed in 1975 by the Cabinet to ignore, and, secondly, stressed the fact that the procedure regarding individual candidates, at various levels of government, extended back to the mid 1940's; — *ibid.*, pp. 4888, 4916, 4975, 5059.

306. H.C. Debates, Vol. 121, p. 560, November 2, 1977.

307. See *ante*, p. 60 and footnote 218.

308. Goyer's endorsation was in the following words: "In forming this group, I am following a principle which is not inconsistent with what was said in the House of Commons on June 26, 1969 by the hon. Leader of the Opposition when the revised report of the Royal Commission on Security was tabled". The functions of the group as enunciated by the Solicitor General, were: (1) to study the nature, origin, and causes of subversive and revolutionary action, its objectives and techniques as well as the measures necessary to protect Canadians from internal threats; (2) to compile and analyze information collected on subversive and revolutionary groups and their activities, to estimate the nature and scope of internal threats to Canadians and to plan for measures to counter these threats; and (3) to advise the Solicitor General of Canada on these matters. "The Group" it was stressed "has no operational duties, they are advisory in nature" — H.C. Debates Vol. VIII, pp. 8026-27, Sept. 21, 1971.

309. H.C. Debates, Vol. X, p. 10639, June 26, 1969.

310 . H.C. Debates, Vol. 121, p. 568, November 2, 1977.

311. *Loc. cit.*

312. *Loc. cit.*

313. The transcript from which the important extracts, quoted in the text above, are taken, was kindly provided by the Prime Minister's office.

314. For an expression of the same thoughts by Mr. Trudeau in the House of Commons, see H.C. Debates, Vol. 121, pp. 563-5, November 2, 1977. The same philosophy is to be found, for example, in the major speech by Francis Fox, Solicitor General at the time, in reply to the Opposition's non-confidence motion based on the government's alleged failure to follow the principle of ministerial responsibility "as it applies to the direction and methods used by the government security forces" — see H.C. Debates, Vol. 121, 877 at pp. 885-6, November 15, 1977.

315. A related problem that occasionally surfaces is the extent to which a government is constitutionally entitled to call upon a police force to produce for its inspection details of political intervention or attempted political intervention in police investigations by the members of a previous Administration. Mr. Pearson, when he was Prime Minister in 1964, and arising out of the events that led to the Dorion Inquiry, instructed the R.C.M.P. to conduct such an examination of its files over the period of the preceding 10 years. The Opposition, led by Mr. Diefenbaker, refused to cooperate and maintained that the Prime Minister's motives were themselves highly suspect. The essentials of this story and its constitutional implications can be found in H.C. Debates, Vol. I, pp. 4627-4631; *Mike, The Memoirs of Lester B. Pearson*, Vol. 3, pp. 187-194; and Diefenbaker's *Memoirs, The Tumultuous Years*, pp. 266-273.

316. See Edwards, "Criminal Law and its Enforcement in a Permissive Society" (1969-70), 12 *Crim. L.Q.* 417 at pp. 424-25.

317. See Minutes of the Proceedings of the Standing Committee on Justice and Legal Affairs, p. 2:17, November 24, 1977, and pp. 3:87 — 88, November 29, 1977.

318. *Ibid.*, at pp. 3.87 and 3.88.

319. *Transcript of Proceedings*, Vol. 127, pp. 19800-2, and see also *Globe & Mail*, July 7, 1979.

320. *Ibid.*, pp. 19795-9.

321. *Ibid.*, pp. 19809, 19820-1.

322. *Ibid.*, pp. 19822, 19824-5.

323. Memorandum on "Domestic security investigation guidelines" dated November 4, 1976, and memorandum on "Guidelines on use of informants" dated December 15, 1976, from Attorney General Edward H. Levi to Clarence M. Kelley, Director, Federal Bureau of Investigation. Both these memoranda were kindly provided by the U.S. Dept. of Justice.

324. See essay cited in footnote 138A at p. 370. There is a similar office, composed of lawyers, in the F.B.I. itself which advises on the legality of the Bureau's operations.

325. See section 3-305. Other agencies, generally regarded as constituting the Intelligence Community within the United States, whose activities are subject to scrutiny by the Attorney General, include the National Security Agency, and intelligence elements within the F.B.I., the military services, the Dept. of Defence, the Dept. of the Treasury, the Dept. of Energy and the Drug Enforcement Administration.

326. *Ibid.*, section 3-403. Reporting of illegalities and improprieties to the President is through the medium of a small, independent group of prominent citizens who constitute the President's Intelligence Oversight Board, which functions within the White House.

327. The main legislative proposal is the National Intelligence Reorganization and Reform Act of 1978, Senate Bill S.2525, commonly known as the Huddleston Bill. This Bill, so far as the F.B.I. is concerned, only extends to its roles in the fields of counter espionage and counter terrorism. It does not deal with the domestic security intelligence activities of the F.B.I. Up to now, only Title III of the Huddleston Bill has been enacted into law, in the form of the Foreign Intelligence Surveillance Act of 1978, Public Law 95-511, 95th Congress.

328. Bill H.R. 5030, incorporating what is being described as the Charter of the United States Federal Bureau of Investigation, was introduced in the House of Representatives on July 31, 1979. If enacted, it will replace the Presidential Executive Order referred to in the text (*supra*, footnote 326). In scope, it purports to govern all the Bureau's investigative and law enforcement functions but does not extend to the F.B.I.'s foreign intelligence and counter-intelligence activities.

329. It is for these reasons that I find unacceptable the views put forward by the present Commissioner of the R.C.M.P. when testifying before the Commons' Standing Committee on Justice and Legal Affairs on November 29, 1977, see *Proceedings*, p. 3:383. Commissioner Simmonds stated on that occasion: "I am more than prepared to be accountable in the sense that I will be accountable for the general management of the force, the expenditure of resources and so on, but I would buck like a steer if anybody tried to tell me who I could investigate and *how I must go about it*" (my italics).

330. On the functioning of the Standing Committees see generally C.E.S. Franks: *Parliament and Security Matters*, 1979, (unpublished paper prepared for the McDonald Commission of Inquiry) pp. 59-67, and J.B. Stewart: *The Canadian House of Commons*, 1977, pp. 157-196.

331. Official Secrets Act, 1973, new section 16(5), enacted under the provisions of the Protection of Privacy Act, Statutes of Canada 1973, c.50, s.6.

332. Speaking in somewhat the same vein, Mr. Justice Hope in his Report of the Royal Commission on Security and Intelligence in Australia writes:

"It has been said often enough and I think it is correct, that the Minister should not be concerned with the details of ASIO's operations and activities. This is a good general rule, but it should not be applied inflexibly ... Some of the cases in which the Minister will want detailed information are already provided for by statute in the Telephonic Communications (Interception) Act 1960-1975. There are doubtless other cases where the sensitivity or difficulty or possible ramifications of an operation will or may be such that the Director General should get ministerial advice or direction. *There has been too great a tendency in the past for ministers to avoid making decisions in security matters properly within their spheres.*'' (My italics).

Fourth Report (Parliamentary Paper No. 248/1977), Vol. 1, pp. 174-175.

333.   It would be helpful if further inquiries were undertaken as to the positions taken by Parliament in other circumstances, such as immigration, deportation, and the investment of foreign capital, where the introduction of different legal criteria has been made an integral part of Canada's statute law.

334.   Hope Commission, *op. cit.*, 4th Report, Vol. 1, p. 39.

335.   *Report of the Royal Commission on Security* (Abridged), 1969, p. 21.

336.   H.C. Debates, Vol. VIII, p. 8027, Sept. 21, 1971.

337.   Mackenzie Report, *op. cit.*, p. 23. Cf. the position in Australia where the right of access to the Prime Minister by the Head of ASIO, the national security and intelligence organisation, has been defined in notably more extensive terms. Thus, under the 1949 Charter of ASIO, inaugurating the Service, the Director General was declared to have "direct access to the Prime Minister at all times." This right was qualified in the 1950 Charter "to all matters of moment affecting security which [the D.G.] think(s) should be considered by or on behalf of the Government as a whole." The Hope Report did not question the continuing applicability of the above understanding. See the *Report of the [Australia]* Royal Commission on Intelligence and Security, (Parliamentary Paper No. 248/1977) Fourth Report, Vol. 1, pp. 163-166.

338.   Hope Commission, *op. cit.*, Fourth Report, Vol. 1, pp. 176-7.

339.   *Op. cit.*, p. 180.

340.   *Op. cit.*, p. 179.

341.   *Op. cit.*, p. 183.